Rand McNally POCKET ROAD ATLAS

United States / Canada / Mexico

Contents

Population figures are Dec. 31, 1986, estimates, as reported by
Market Statistics, S & M M 1987 "Survey of Buying Power."

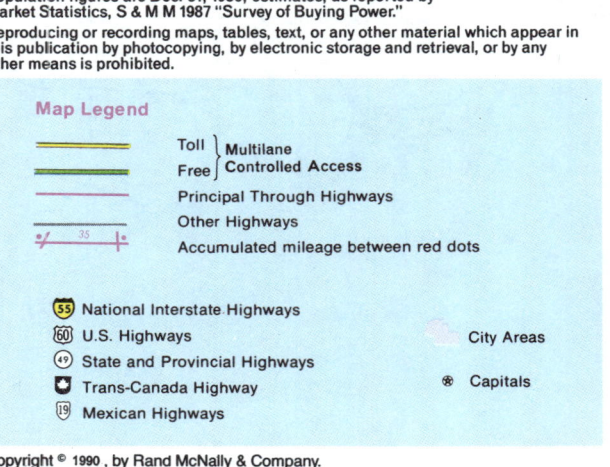

Map Legend

Toll ⎱ Multilane
Free ⎰ Controlled Access

Principal Through Highways

Other Highways

35 Accumulated mileage between red dots

55 National Interstate Highways

60 U.S. Highways

49 State and Provincial Highways

Trans-Canada Highway

19 Mexican Highways

City Areas

⊛ Capitals

0 100 200 300 400 miles
CAN
WASHINGTON
Seattle
Olympia
Spokane
Portland
Salem
OREGON
MONTANA
Missoula
Great Falls
Helena
Butte
Billings
NORTH DAKOTA
Bismarck
Fargo
SOUTH DAKOTA
Rapid City
Sioux Falls
WYOMING
Boise
Idaho Falls
Pocatello
IDAHO
CALIFORNIA
NEVADA
Casper
NEBRASKA
UTAH
Cheyenne
Salt Lake City
COLORADO
Reno
Oakland
Sacramento
San Francisco
Denver
Lincoln
KANSAS
Colorado Springs
Pueblo
Wichita
Las Vegas
ARIZONA
NEW MEXICO
OKLAHOMA
Santa Fe
TEXAS
Amarillo
Oklahoma City
Los Angeles
Albuquerque
San Diego
Phoenix
Lubbock
Fort Worth
Tucson
Nogales
El Paso
Abilene
Austin
San Antonio
Laredo
Corpus Christi
MEXICO

UNITED STATES
Interstate Highways

Tollways
Freeways
under construction
or proposed

4/ALABAMA

0 10 20 30 40 50 miles

TENN.

MISS.

Corinth
Iuka
Fulton
Fulton

Florence
Sheffield
Tuscumbia
Russellville
Muscle Shoals
Town Creek
Moulton
Hartselle
Haleyville
Hamilton
Winfield
Vernon
Jasper
Fayette
Reform
Columbus
Aliceville
Northport
Tuscaloosa

St Joseph
Pickwick L.
Athens
Decatur
Laceys Sprs.
Cullman
Oneonta

Huntsville
Scottsboro
Stevenson
Bridgeport
S. Pittsburg
Chattanooga
Jasper

GA.

Dalton
Rome
Cartersville
Cedartown

Arab
Albertville
Boaz
Guntersville
Ft Payne
Centre
Attalla
Gadsden
Piedmont
Jacksonville
Ashville
Anniston
Oxford
Carrollton

Birmingham
Fairfield
Bessemer
Tarrant City
Leeds
Homewood
Pell City
Talladega
Winterboro
Lineville
Childersburg
Sylacauga
Roanoke
La Grange
West Point
Lanett
Opelika
Auburn
Columbus

Brent
Clanton
Alexander City
Lafayette
Dadeville

Eutaw
Greensboro
Marion
Uniontown
Demopolis
York
Linden
Selma
Prattville
Wetumpka
Tallassee
Montgomery
Tuskegee
Phenix City

Butler
Thomasville
Camden
Greenville
Troy
Brundidge
Clio
Abbeville
Eufaula

Jackson
Frisco City
Monroeville
McKenzie
Evergreen
Andalusia
Opp
Elba
Ozark
Enterprise
Headland
Dothan
Blakely

Chatom
Mt. Vernon
Brewton
Atmore
East Brewton
Florala
Luverne
Union Sprs.

FLA.

Saraland
Prichard
Bay Minette
Stapleton
Milton
Crestview
De Funiak Sprs.
Chipley
Marianna

Mobile
Fairhope
Foley
Gulf Shores
Mobile Bay
Pensacola
Ft. Walton Beach
Panama City

GULF OF MEXICO

©R. MSN.

90/1

0   70   140 miles

ARCTIC OCEAN

Barrow
Wainwright
Prudhoe Bay
Deadhorse
Sagwon
Umiat
Point Hope
Beaufort Sea
Inuvik

CHUKCHI PENINSULA
USSR
Rene

Chevgun

Cape Krusenstern Nat'l Mon.
Kotzebue
Kobuk Valley Nat'l Park
Wiseman
Rampart House
Gates of the Arctic Nat'l Park

Ft. Good Hope
Ft. Norman

Nome
Teller
Livengood
Fort Yukon
Circle
Eagle
Keno
NW TERR

St. Lawrence Island
Savoonga
Unalakleet
Tofty
Nenana
Fairbanks
Boundary
Dawson
YUKON

Alakanuk
Kotlik
McGrath
McKinley Park
Big Delta
Tok Junction
Minto
Whitehorse
Watson Lake

Hooper Bay
Paxson
Koidern
Kluane
Haines Junction

Nunivak I.
Bethel
Kwethluk
Anchorage
Palmer
Chugach
Glennallen
Wrangell St. Elias Nat'l Park
Teslin
B.C.
Dease Lake

Kenai
Soldotna
Valdez
Cordova
Haines
Skagway
Juneau
Telegraph Cr.

Newhalem
Seward
Yakutat
Hoonah

Dillingham
Homer
Port Graham
Kenai Fjords Nat'l Park
Glacier Bay Nat'l Park
Sitka
Petersburg
Wrangell

BERING SEA
Naknek
Katmai Nat'l Park
GULF OF ALASKA

Kodiak
Port Heiden
Chignik
Aniakchak Nat'l Mon.

Dutch Harbor
Unimak
Unimak I.

ALEUTIAN ISLANDS
Attu
Attu I.
Rat Is.
Andreanof Is.
Atka
Fort Glenn
Umnak I.

---

0   150   300 miles

KAUAI
Kilauea
Haena
Kekaha
Kapaa
Lihue
Puuwai
Koloa
Kalaheo
Kahaino
NIIHAU

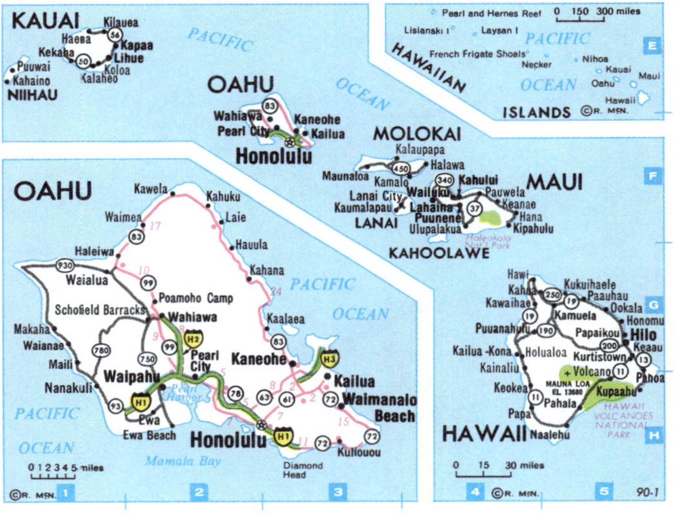

Pearl and Hermes Reef
Lisianski I.
Laysan I.
French Frigate Shoals
Necker
Nihoa
Kauai
Maui
Oahu
Hawaii
HAWAIIAN ISLANDS

OAHU
Wahiawa
Kaneohe
Pearl City
Kailua
Honolulu

MOLOKAI
Kalaupapa
Maunaloa
Kamalo
Halawa
Kualapuu
Kahului
Wailuku
Pauwela
MAUI
Lanai City
Lahaina
Keanae
Hana
Kaumalapau
Puunene
Kipahulu
Ulupalakua
LANAI
KAHOOLAWE

OAHU
Kawela
Kahuku
Waimea
Laie
Haleiwa
Hauula
Waialua
Kahana
Poamoho Camp
Schofield Barracks
Wahiawa
Kaalaea
Makaha
Waianae
Maili
Nanakuli
Waipahu
Pearl City
Kaneohe
Kailua
Waimanalo Beach
Ewa
Ewa Beach
Honolulu
Kuliouou
Diamond Head
Mamala Bay

0 1 2 3 4 5 miles

Hawi
Kukuihaele
Kahala
Paauhau
Kamuela
Ookala
Honomu
Puuanahulu
Papaikou
Hilo
Kailua-Kona
Kurtistown
Keaau
Kainaliu
Holualoa
Volcano
Phoa
Keokea
Pahala
HAWAII VOLCANOES NATIONAL PARK
MAUNA LOA EL. 13680
Papa
HAWAII
Naalehu

0   15   30 miles

90-1

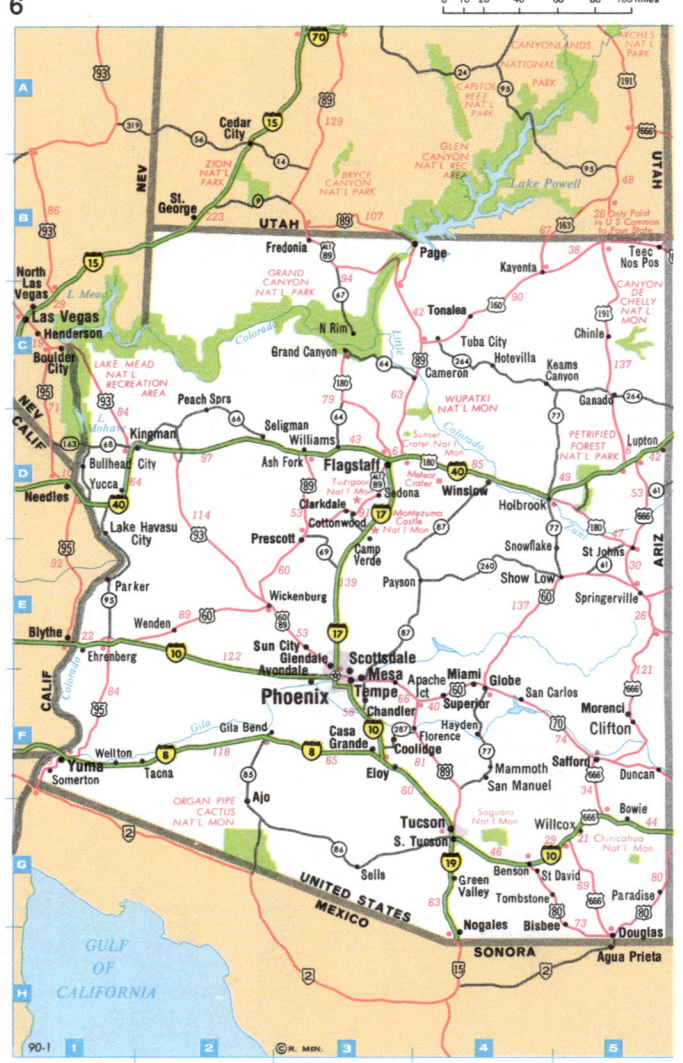

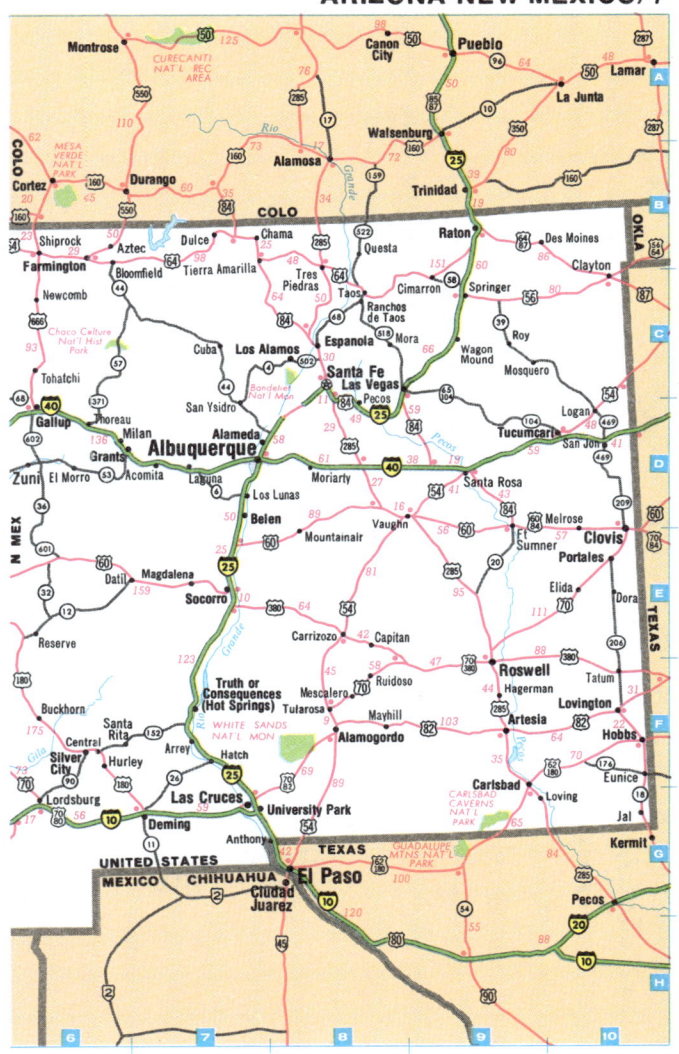

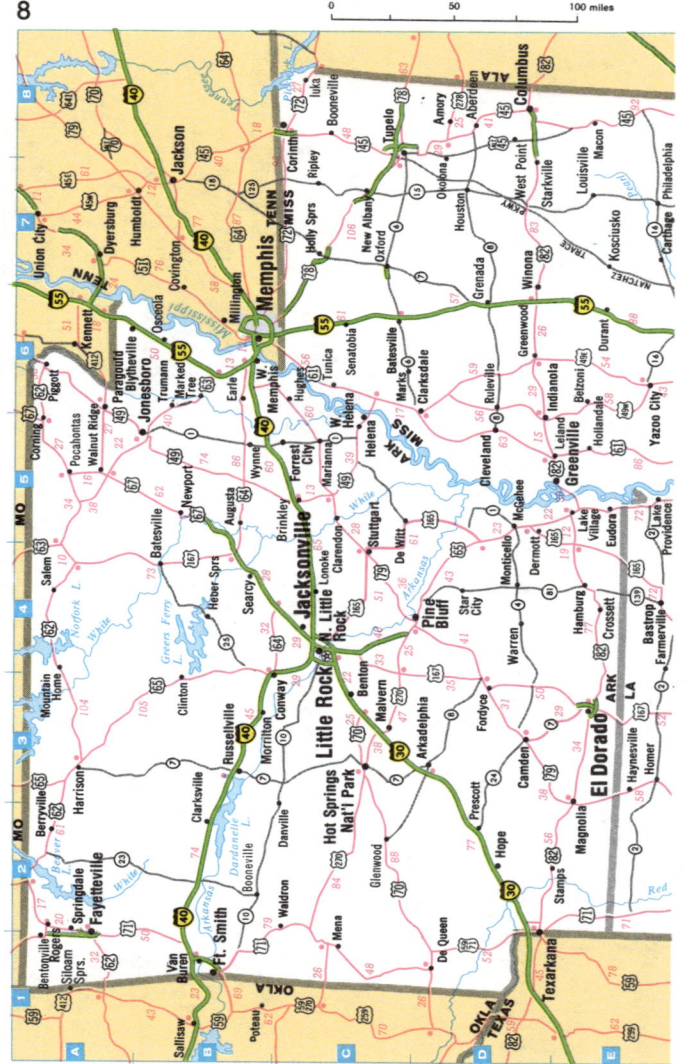

8

0   50   100 miles

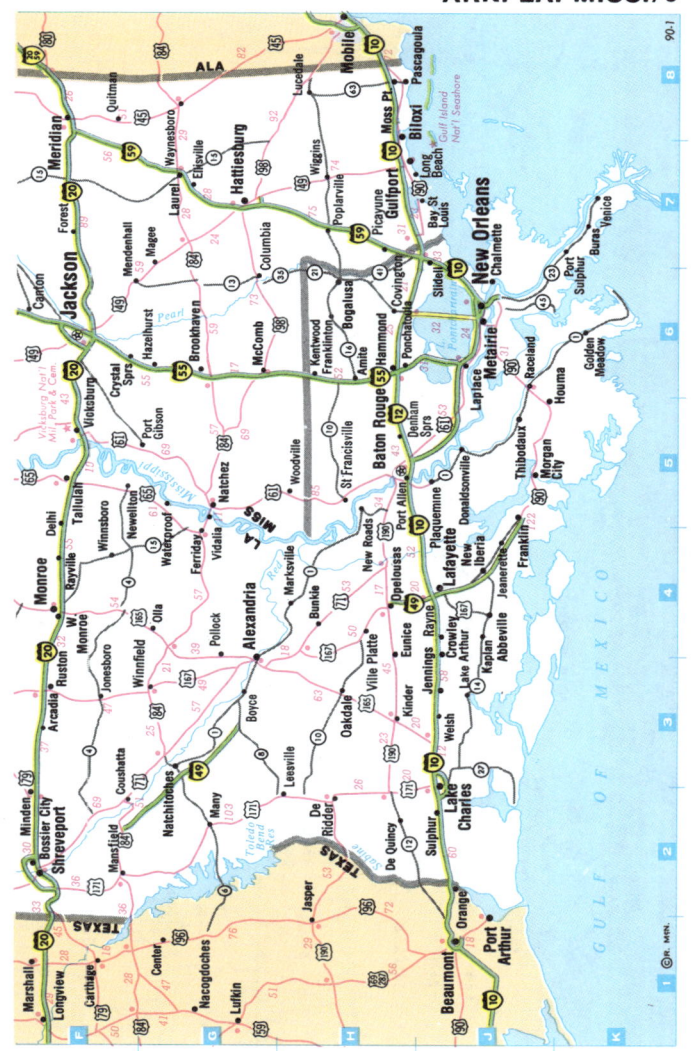

0 25 50 75 100 miles

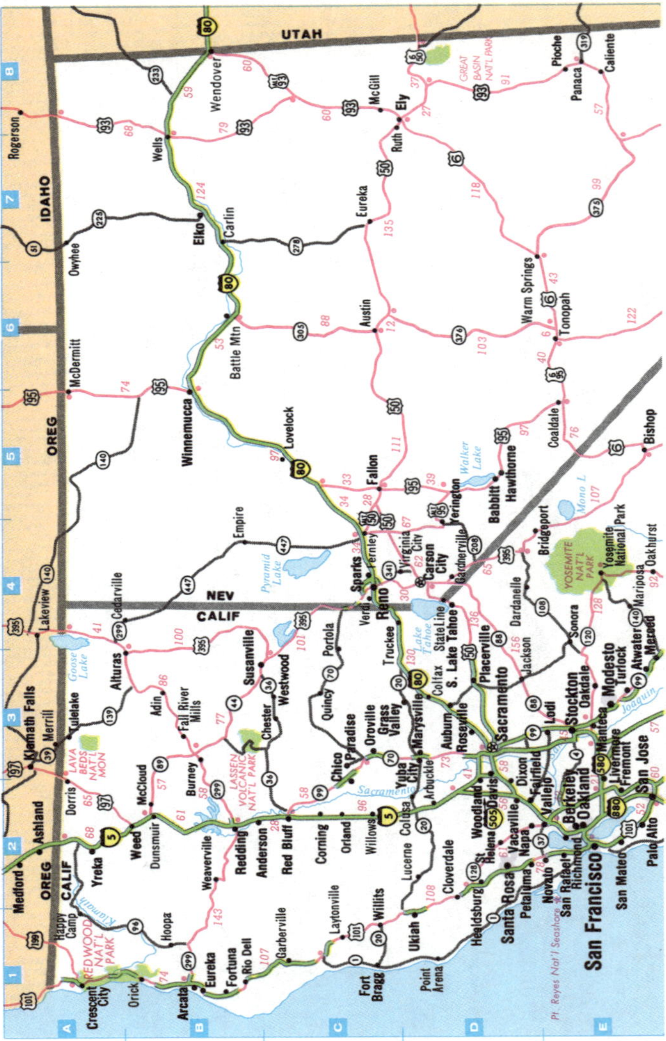

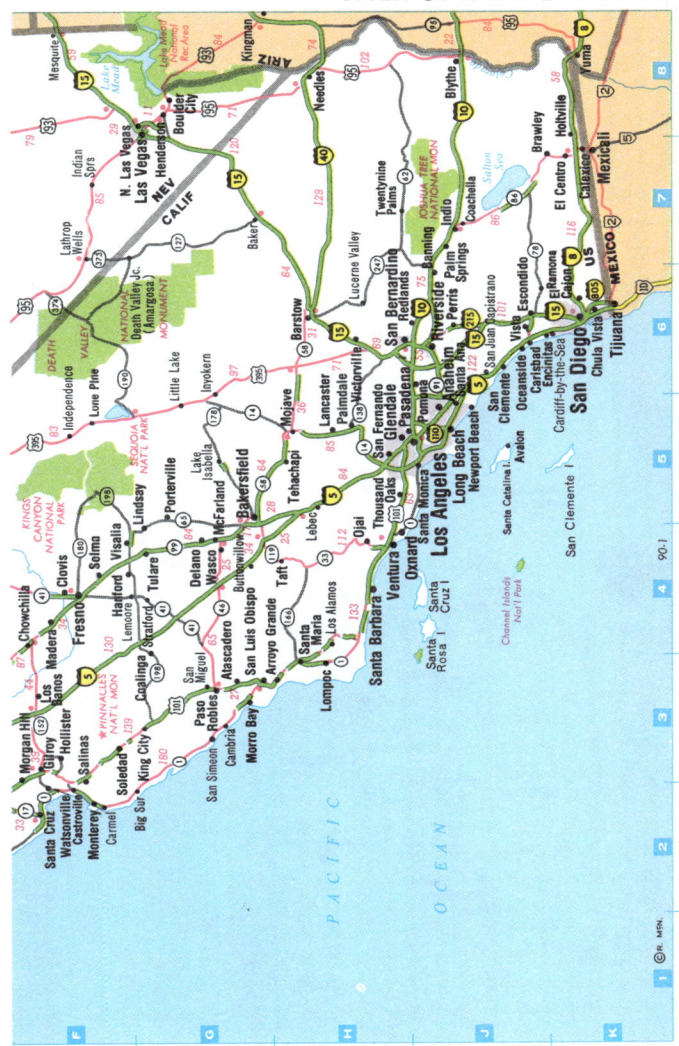

0 5 10 15 20 25 miles

Hudson

NY
VT

7

Troy
87
Albany
90

VT

Bennington

Williamstown
Adams
N.
Adams
Dalton
Pittsfield
Lenox
Lee
20
90
21

Great
Barrington
23

Canaan

Shelburn Falls
44
2

Deerfield

Northampton

Holyoke
Chicopee
20
90

Westfield
W. Springfield

Brattleboro
Keene
101
12

Winchendon

Greenfield
91

Athol
Gardner
Leomins

Barre

Amherst

Quabbin
Res.
122

Ware

Palmer
202
MASSACHUSETTS
Spencer
90

Springfield
20
MASS

Auburn
Southbridge
Webster

CONN

Winsted
Simsbury
Torrington
Litchfield
Watertown
New
Milford
Danbury
84
6

Windsor
Locks
202

Windsor

Hartford
W. Hartford

Bristol
New
Britain
Waterbury
691

Enfield

84

Putnam
131

E.
Manchester
Hartford

Storrs
384

Danielson
44
444

Moosup
395

Willimantic

Middletown
Meriden
Naugatuck
91
Wallingford

Seymour Hamden
Ansonia
Shelton
Trumbull
Norwalk
Bridgeport
Fairfield
Stamford
Greenwich
95
684

Danbury

New Haven Guilford Clinton
Milford
Stratford

Gov. John D. Lodge
95

Norwich
138

Groton
New
London
Mystic

LONG   ISLAND   SOUND

Greenport

Riverhead
Southampton
Montauk

495

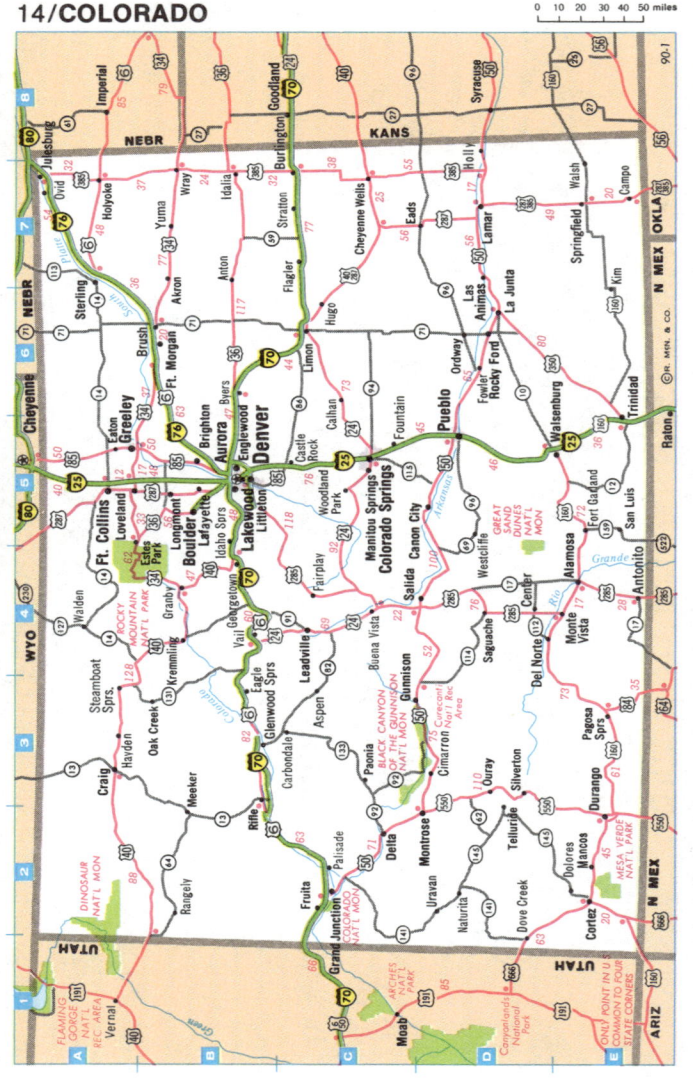

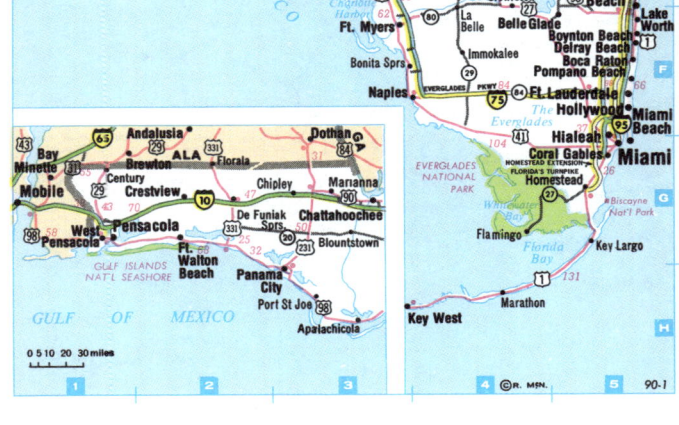

0 10 20 40 60 80 miles

Moultrie · Waycross · 50 · Brunswick
Bainbridge · 19 · Cumberland Island Nat'l Seashore
Thomasville · Homerville · ATLANTIC
Chattahoochee · Valdosta · 84 · 36 · Folkston · 95
Quincy · GA · Monticello · Jasper · 441 · Jacksonville
Tallahassee · Madison · 90 · Macclenny · Jacksonville Beach
Crawfordville · Live Oak · Green · 50
Perry · Lake · Cove · St. Augustine
Carrabelle · City · Sprs · Castillo de San Marcos Nat'l Mon
Branford · High · Starke · OCEAN
Springs · Gainesville
Chiefland · Palatka
Williston · Bunnell · Ormond Beach
Ocala · Daytona Beach
De Land · New Smyrna Beach
Inverness · Leesburg · Canaveral Nat'l Seashore
Brooksville · Sanford · Winter · John F Kennedy Space Center
Winter Garden · Park · Titusville
Clermont · Orlando · Cape Canaveral
New Port Richey · BEE LINE · Cocoa
Tarpon Sprs · Walt Disney World/Epcot Center · Kissimmee · St Cloud · Melbourne
Dunedin · Lakeland · Winter · Haven
Clearwater · Plant · Lake Wales
Tampa · City · Bartow
St. Petersburg · Fort Meade · Vero Beach
Wauchula · Ft. Pierce
Bradenton · Avon Park
Sarasota · Sebring · Stuart
Arcadia · Lake · FLORIDA
Venice · Placid · West
Port Charlotte · Okeechobee · Palm · Riviera Beach
Punta Gorda · Lake Okeechobee · Beach · Lake Worth
Ft. Myers · Clewiston · Boynton Beach
Bonita Sprs · La Belle · Belle Glade · Delray Beach · Boca Raton
Naples · Immokalee · Pompano Beach
EVERGLADES PKWY · Ft. Lauderdale
The Everglades · Hollywood · Miami Beach
Hialeah · Miami
Coral Gables · HOMESTEAD EXTENSION FLORIDA'S TURNPIKE
EVERGLADES NATIONAL PARK · Homestead
Whitewater Bay · Biscayne Nat'l Park
Flamingo · Florida Bay · Key Largo
Key West · Marathon

Inset map:

0 5 10 20 30 miles

Andalusia · Dothan
Bay Minette · Brewton · Florala · ALA
Mobile · Century · Crestview · Chipley · Marianna
West Pensacola · Pensacola · De Funiak Sprs · Chattahoochee
Ft. Walton Beach · Blountstown
GULF ISLANDS NAT'L SEASHORE · Panama City
Port St Joe
GULF OF MEXICO · Apalachicola

1 2 3 4 © R. MᶜN. 5 90-1

0 10 20 30 40 50 miles

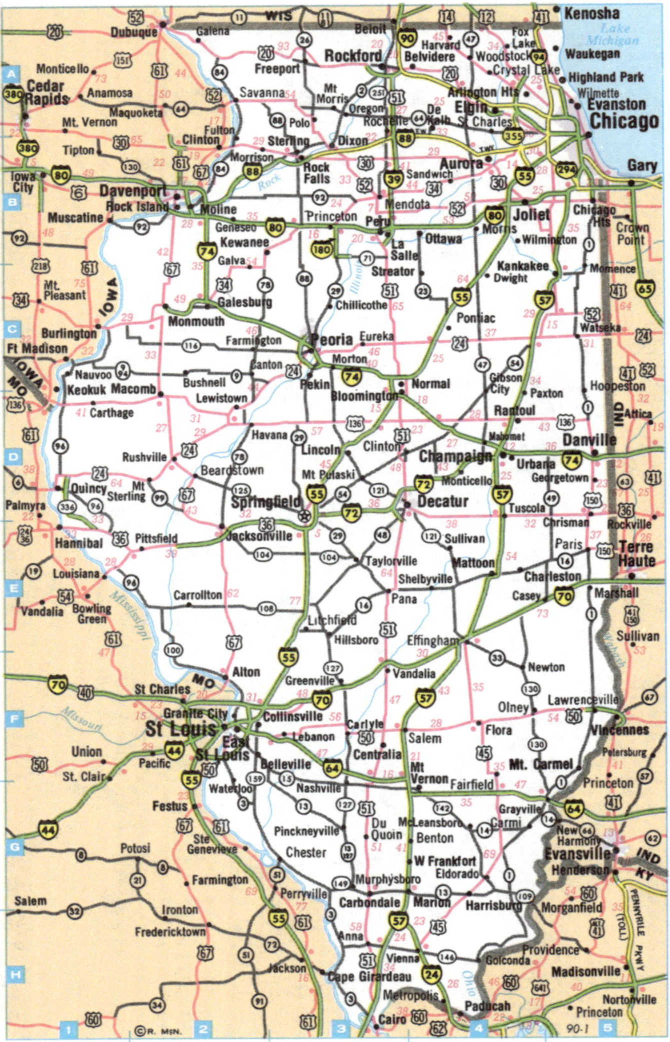

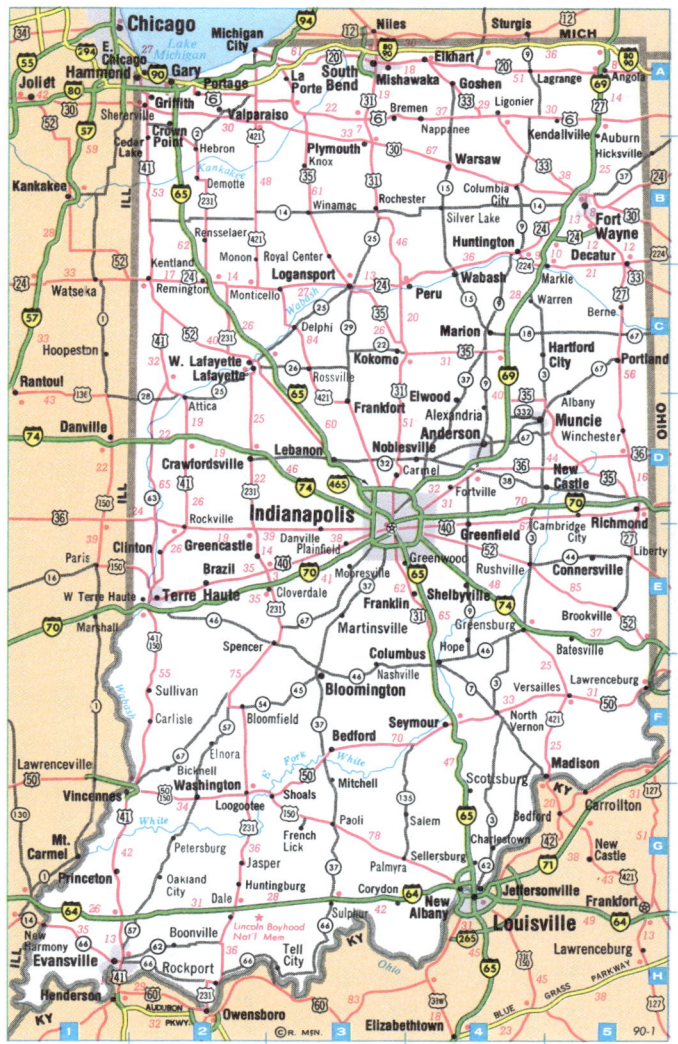

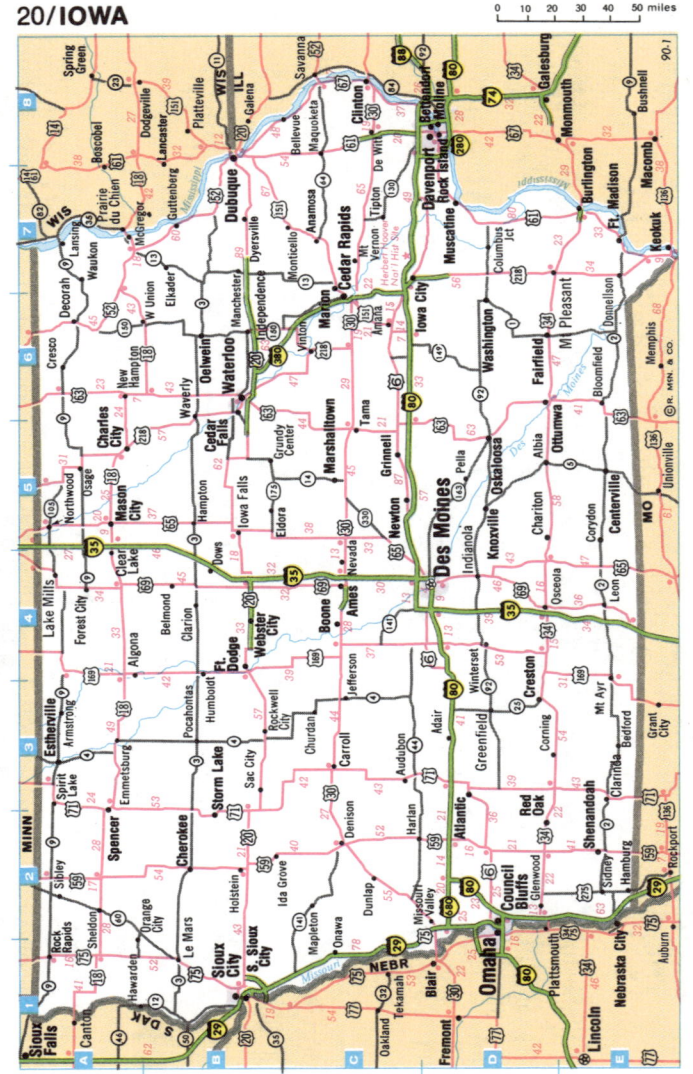

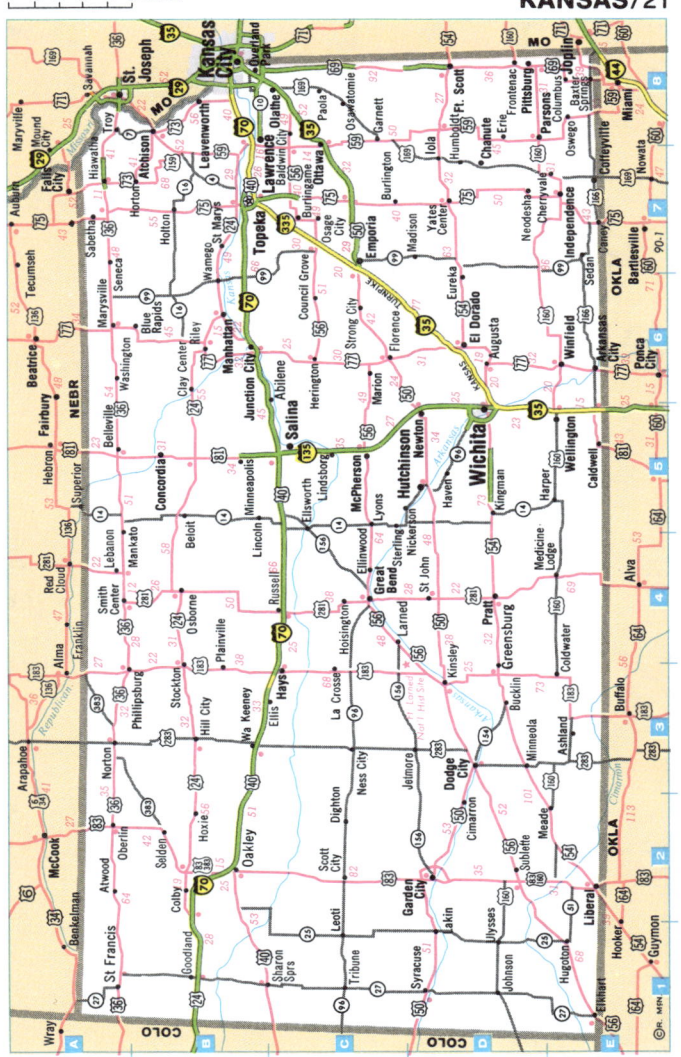

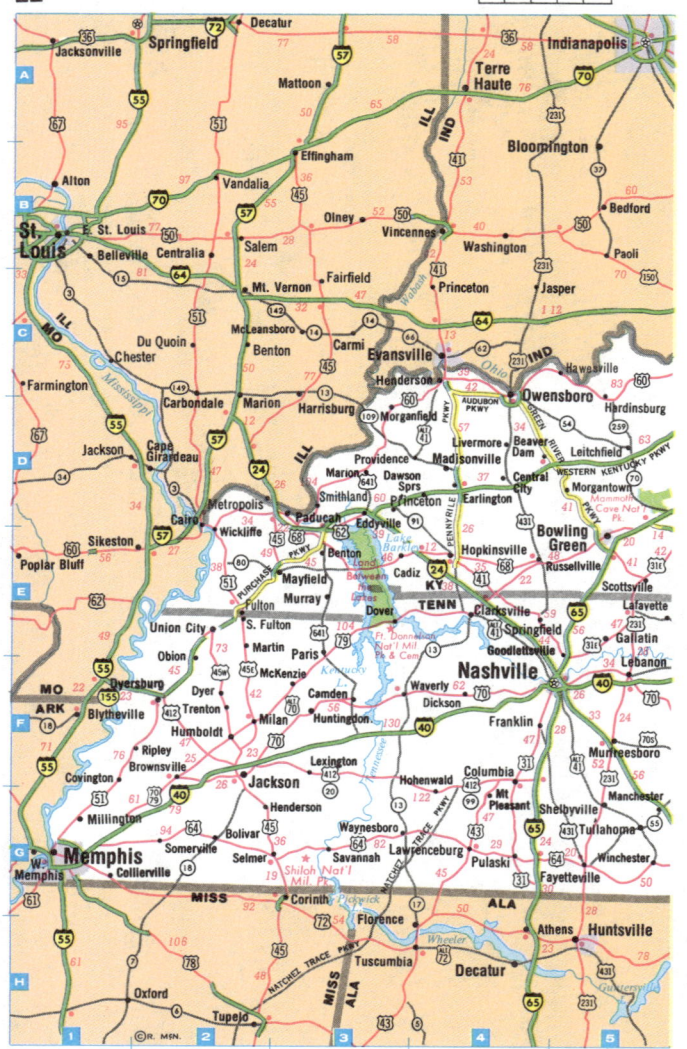

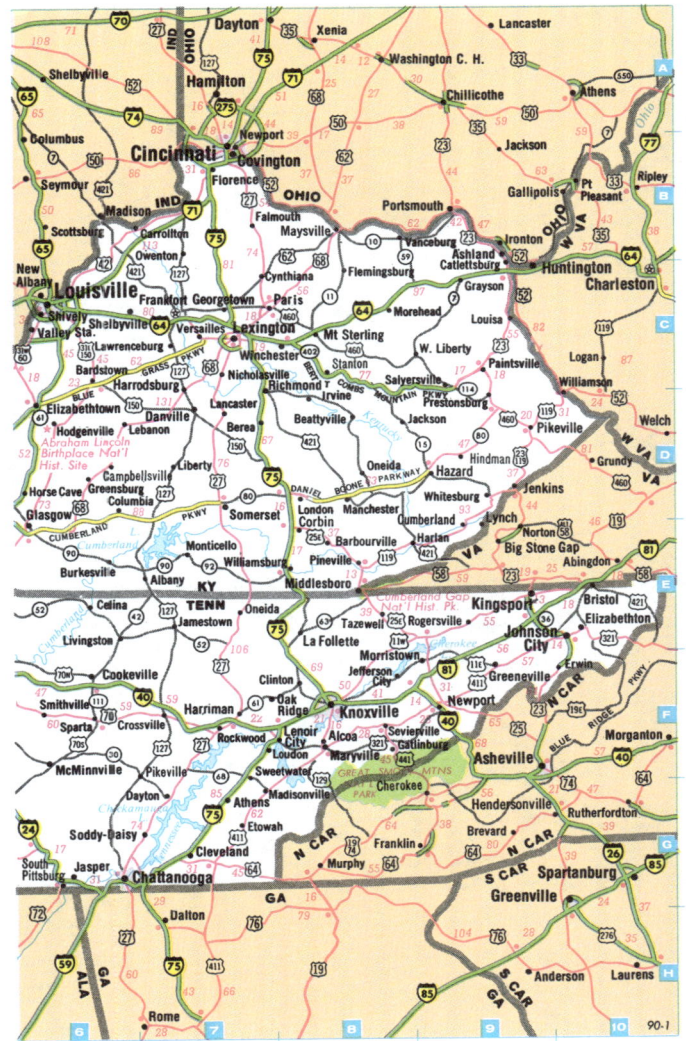

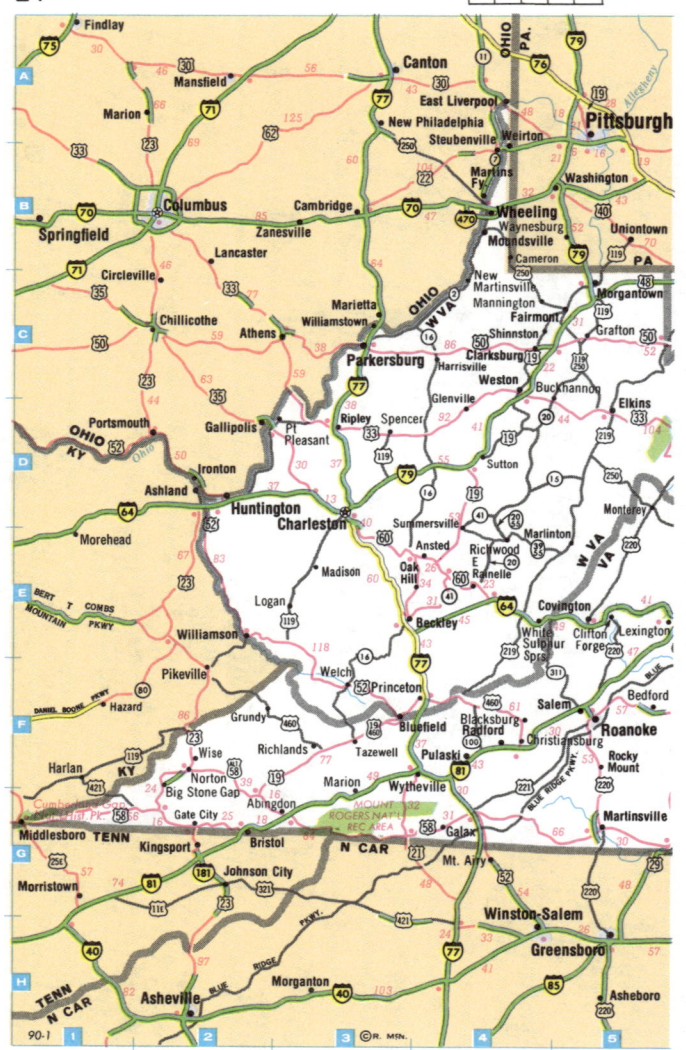

0 10 20 30 40 50 **miles**

Findlay
75
Mansfield
30
Marion
71
71
33
23
69
Springfield
Columbus
70
70
Zanesville
Cambridge
85
Circleville
71
35
33
77
Chillicothe
59
Athens
Marietta
Williamstown
50
Portsmouth
52
OHIO
KY
Ohio
50
Gallipolis
Ironton
Ashland
64
Huntington
Charleston
52
Morehead
67
83
23
Logan
Madison
60
119
Williamson
118
Pikeville
80
Hazard
86
Harlan
119
23
Wise
KY
421
Norton
Big Stone Gap
24
Middlesboro TENN
Gate City
58
Morristown
Kingsport
Bristol
57
74
81
181
Johnson City
321
114
23
40
97
TENN
N CAR
Asheville
82
Morganton
40
BLUE RIDGE
103

Canton
11
OHIO
PA.
79
76
30
East Liverpool
77
New Philadelphia
Steubenville
250
60
Martins Fy.
22
Washington
Cambridge
70
470
Wheeling
47
Waynesburg
Moundsville
Cameron
79
Uniontown
New
Martinsville
250
Morgantown
48
Mannington
Fairmont
Shinnston
86
Clarksburg
19
Grafton
Parkersburg
77
Harrisville
Weston
Buckhannon
Ripley
Spencer
Glenville
92
Elkins
33
219
118
79
20
44
219
104
16
Sutton
15
250
Monterey
41
22
Marlinton
Summersville
Ansted
Richwood
E.
Oak
Ranelle
Hill
60
W VA
VA
Beckley
45
41
64
Covington
31
White
Clifton
Lexington
Welch
Sulphur
Forge
220
16
52
Princeton
Sprse
311
BLUE
77
460
61
Salem
Bedford
Grundy
460
Blacksburg
Bluefield
Radford
Christiansburg
Roanoke
Richlands
100
Pulaski
Rocky
Tazewell
81
43
Mount
Marion
49
Wytheville
90
220
Abingdon
16
Martinsville
MOUNT
ROGERS NAT
31
REC AREA
58
Galax
53
66
N CAR
21
Mt. Airy
52
220
48
48
29
Winston-Salem
23
421
PKWY.
24
33
77
Greensboro
57
85
Asheboro

90-1
1
2
3
©R. M&N.
4
5

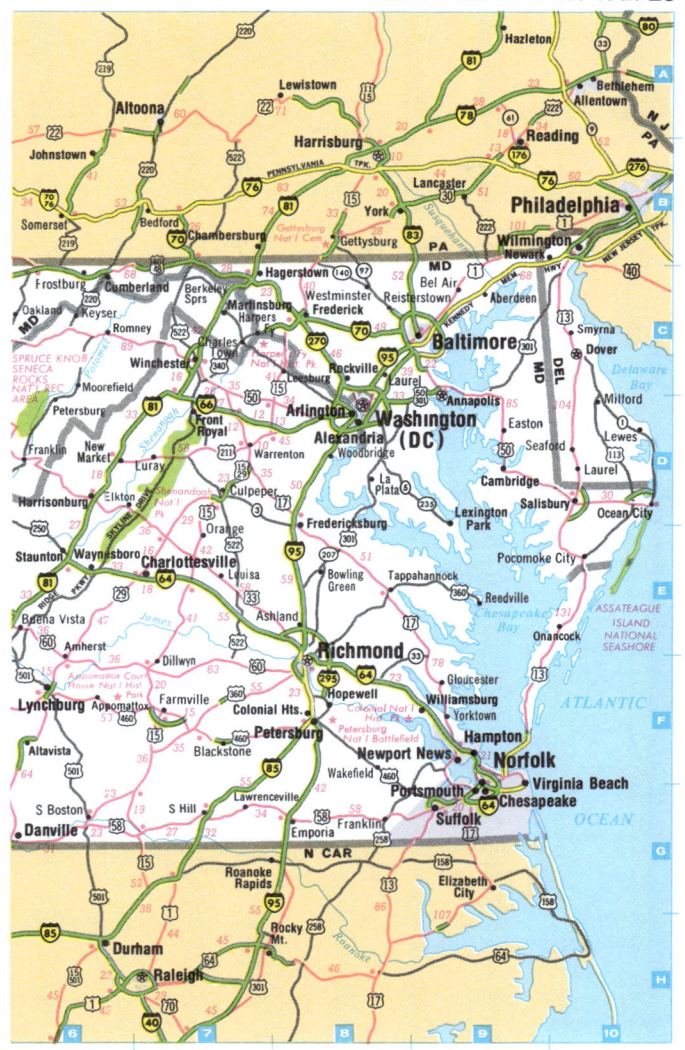

0 10 20 30 40 50 miles
Baie St Paul
St Lawrence
St. Anne du Beaupre
Lauzon
Montmagny
St. Pamphile
QUE
N B
Edmundston
Madawaska
Fort Kent
Van Buren
Grand Falls
St Quentin
Allagash
Eagle Lake
Caribou
Fort Fairfield
Presque Isle
Ashland
Mars Hill
CANADA
U S
St John
Hartland
Woodstock
Houlton
Patten
Chamberlain Lake
Beauceville
Ville St. Georges
CANADA
UNITED STATES
Moosehead Lake
Jackman
Lac Megantic
Millinocket
Penobscot
Danforth
Vanceboro
Mattawamkeag
Greenville
Brownville Jct
Lincoln
Dover-Foxcroft
Howland
St Stephan
Calais
St Croix
Stratton
Guilford
Bingham
Kingfield
Rangeley
Dexter
Old Town
Orono
Eastport
Lubec
Newport
Bangor
Brewer
Madison
Skowhegan
Pittsfield
Hampden
Machias
Farmington
Fairfield
Bucksport
Mexico
Waterville
Winslow
Ellsworth
Milbridge
Bethel
Rumford
Livermore Falls
Belfast
Searsport
Bar Harbor
ACADIA NAT'L PARK
Winthrop
Augusta
Norway
Lewiston
Auburn
Gardiner
Waldoboro
Camden
Rockland
Thomaston
Kennebec
TPK
Fryeburg
Bath
Wiscasset
Acadia Nat'l Park
N Windham
Cornish
Brunswick
Yarmouth
Boothbay Harbor
Westbrook
Portland
MAINE
Old Orchard Beach
Saco
Biddeford
Sanford
Kennebunk
Rochester
Ogunquit
York Beach
Dover
Kittery
Portsmouth
Newburyport
NH
ATLANTIC OCEAN
©R. McN.
90-1

ISLE ROYALE
NAT'L PARK
Lake Superior

0 10 20 30 40 50 miles

0 10 20 40 miles

LAKE SUPERIOR

LAKE

Copper Harbor
Laurium
Hancock
Houghton
Ontonagon
Baraga
L'Anse
Negaunee
Ishpeming
Bergland
Ironwood
Wakefield
Watersmeet
Hurley
WIS
Iron River
Eagle River
Iron Mountain
Norway
Menominee
Marinette

Negaunee
Marquette
Ishpeming
Munising
Pictured Rocks Nat'l Lakeshore
Sault Ste. Marie
Sault Ste. Marie
ONT.
CANADA
U.S.
Newberry
Rudyard
De Tour Village
Drummond

Rapid River
Gladstone
Escanaba
Manistique
St Ignace
Mackinaw City
Mackinac Island
Bois Blanc I.
Cheboygan

Green Bay
Stephenson
Washington I.
Menominee
Sister Bay
Marinette
North Manitou I.
South Manitou I.
Sturgeon Bay
Sleeping Bear Sand Dunes Nat'l Lakeshore
WIS
Kewaunee

Beaver Island
Petoskey
Charlevoix
Grand Traverse Bay
Rogers City
Onaway
Alpena
Thunder Bay
Gaylord
Atlanta
Mancelona
Elk Rapids
Traverse City
Interlochen
Kalkaska
Grayling
Mio
Harrisville
Oscoda
Frankfort
Kingsley
Manton
Roscommon
W Branch
Tawas City

Manistee
Cadillac
Lake City
Marion
Houghton Lake
Gladwin
Standish
Port Austin
Caseville
Bad Axe
Harbor Beach
Ludington
Baldwin
Reed City
Harrison
Clare
Pinconning
Sebewaing
Scottville
Hart
White Cloud
Big Rapids
Mount Pleasant
Midland
Bay City
Saginaw
Sandusky
Whitehall
Muskegon
Sparta
Howard City
Alma
St Louis
Ithaca
Stanton
Chesaning
Burton
Lapeer
Port Huron
Lexington
Grand Haven
Greenville
Ionia
Owosso
Flint
Tlmay City
Romeo
Marysville
Hudsonville
Zeeland
Holland
Kentwood
Grand Rapids
Lowell
Portland
St Johns
Corunna
Fenton
Pontiac
Mt Clemens
Saugatuck
Allegan
Grand Ledge
Hastings
Charlotte
Lansing
Howell
Birmingham
Livonia
Dearborn
Warren
Detroit
Windsor
Plainwell
Battle Creek
Mason
Leslie
Albion
Ann Arbor
Ypsilanti
Trenton
Leamington
S Haven
Otsego
Kalamazoo
Benton Hts.
Benton Harbor
St. Joseph
Marshall
Portage
Jackson
Saline
Adrian
Monroe
Paw Paw
Union City
Three Rivers
Coldwater
Hillsdale
Hudson
Blissfield
Port Clinton
Berrien Sprs
Cassopolis
Sturgis
Gary
Michigan City
South Bend
Elkhart
Goshen
Angola
IND
OHIO
Toledo
Sandusky
Valparaiso
Plymouth
Bowling Green
Maumee

LAKE HURON
LAKE MICHIGAN
Saginaw Bay
LAKE ERIE
Lake St. Clair
ONT. CAN

90-1
©R. MSN.

0 10 20 30 40 50 miles

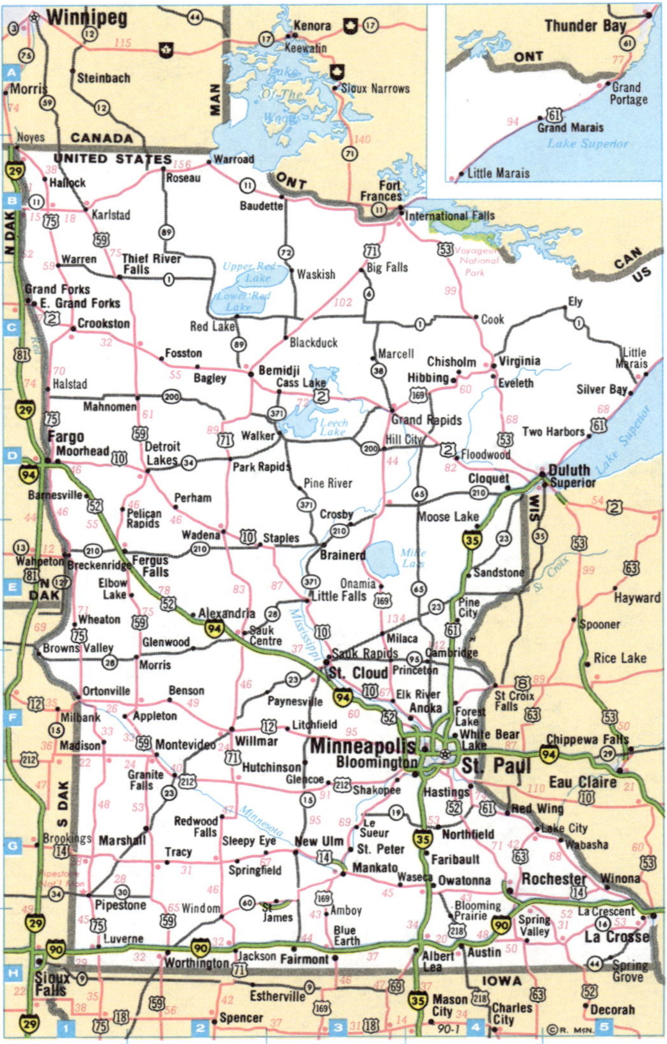

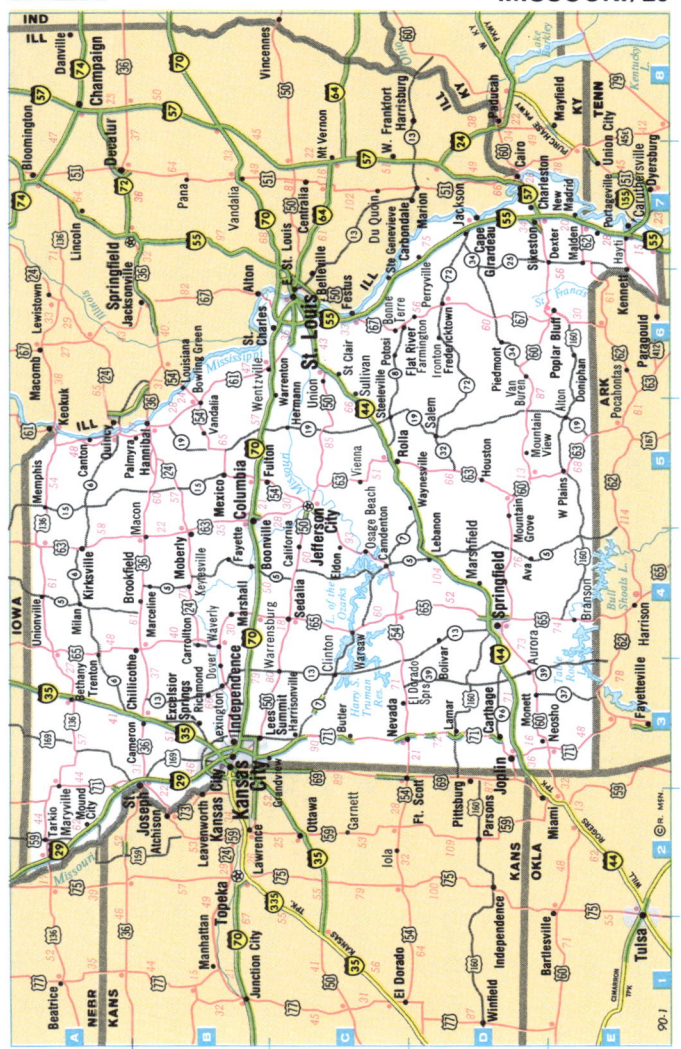

0 10 20 30 40 50 miles

0 10 20 30 40 50 60 70 miles

S DAK

N DAK

Williston

Beach

Glendive

Wibaux

Baker

Ekalaka

Broadus

WYO

Sundance

Plentywood

Culbertson

Sidney

Poplar

Terry

Miles City

Forsyth

Custer Battlefield National Monument

Sheridan

Gillette

Scobey

Wolf Point

Circle

Hardin

Crow Agency

Lodge Grass

Buffalo

Rockglen

Glasgow

Jordan

Winnett

Billings

Laurel

Bridger

Greybull

Powell

Cody

SASK

Malta

Fort Peck Lake

Harlem

Chinook

Lewistown

Roundup

Columbus

Red Lodge

Lovell

Havre

Big Sandy

Stanford

Harlowton

Big Timber

Livingston

Gardiner

YELLOWSTONE NATIONAL PARK

Rudyard

Chester

Ft Benton

Eagle

Belt

White Sulphur Sprs

Townsend

Three Forks

Manhattan

Belgrade

Bozeman

Shelby

Dutton

Black Eagle

Cascade

Helena

Boulder

Whitehall

Ennis

Sunburst

Cut Bank

Conrad

Choteau

Fairfield

Augusta

Great Falls

Butte

Dillon

Cardston

ALTA

Browning

Deer Lodge

Anaconda

Drummond

Stevensville

Philipsburg

Hamilton

Salmon

Eureka

Libby

Troy

Whitefish

Hungry Horse

Columbia Falls

Kalispell

Somers

Polson

Ronan

St Ignatius

Milltown

Missoula

Superior

Thompson Falls

Plains

St Regis

Wallace

GLACIER INTERNATIONAL PEACE PARK

Flathead Lake

IDAHO

B C

CANADA

UNITED STATES

Milk River

Missouri

Yellowstone

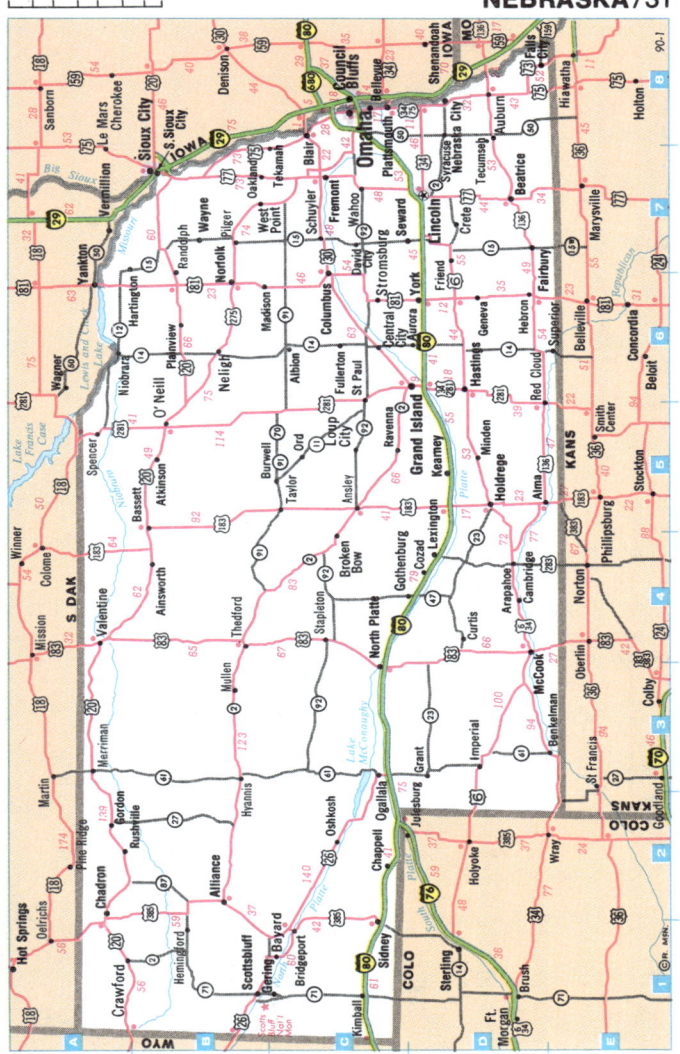

0 10 20 30 40 50 60 70 miles

St. Jean
Granby
Sherbrooke
Cowansville
Magog
Coaticook
Stewartstown
Colebrook
Errol
St. Albans
Swanton
Richford
N. Troy
Newport
Island Pond
N Stratford
Groveton
Berlin
Gorham
Enosburg Falls
Plattsburgh
South Hero
Winooski
Burlington
Essex Jct.
Shelburne
Johnson
Hardwick
Stowe
Lyndonville
Lancaster
Whitefield
Littleton
Waterbury
Marshfield
St. Johnsbury
Montpelier
Barre
Franconia
Woodsville
Lisbon
Bartlett
North Conway
Conway
Fryeburg
Northfield
Middlebury
Randolph
Bradford
N. Woodstock
Warren
Vergennes
Ticonderoga
Brandon
Fair Haven
Whitehall
Poultney
Granville
Rutland
Norwich
White River Jct.
Woodstock
Hanover
Lebanon
Ashland
Plymouth
Center Ossipee
Cornish
Meredith
Windsor
Ludlow
Springfield
Claremont
Newport
New London
Franklin
Laconia
Alton
Farmington
Sanford
Chester
Bellows Falls
Concord
Pittsfield
Rochester
Dover
Kittery
Manchester
Arlington
Putney
Keene
Henniker
Hillsborough
Manchester
Durham
Portsmouth
Epping
Exeter
Hampton
Bennington
Wilmington
Brattleboro
Jaffrey
Milford
Derry
Salem
Newburyport
Haverhill
Williamstown
N. Adams
Winchester
Winchendon
Nashua
Lowell
Lawrence
Greenfield
Fitchburg
Lynn
Woburn
Pittsfield
Northampton
Leominster
Worcester
Boston
Quincy

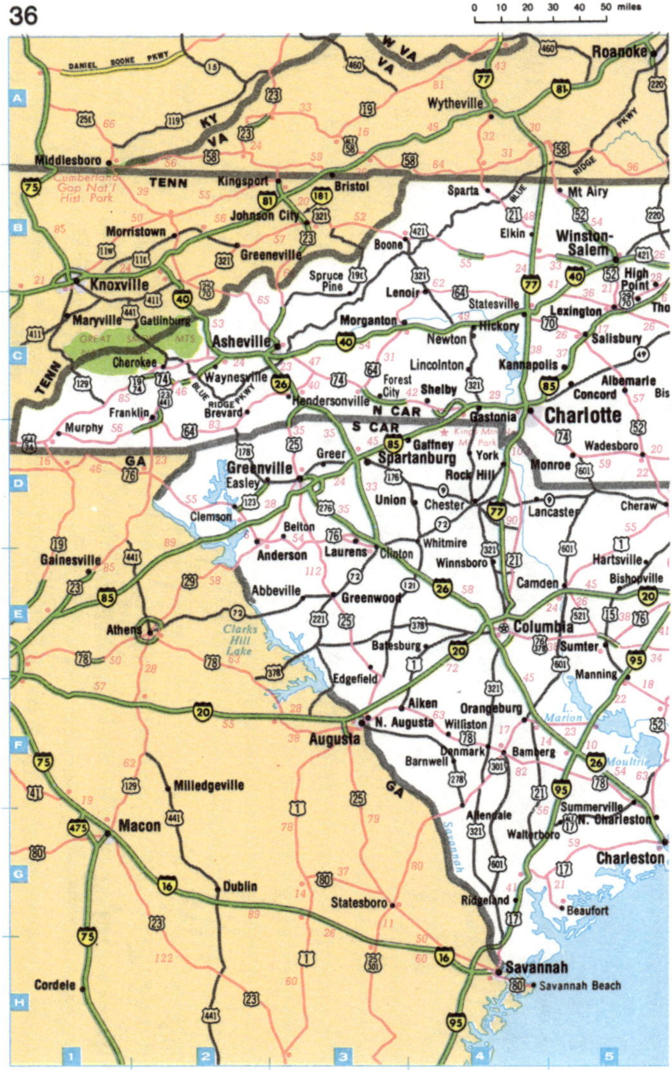

0 10 20 30 40 50 miles

DANIEL BOONE PKWY

W VA
VA
KY
VA
TENN
GA
N CAR
S CAR

Roanoke
Wytheville
Middlesboro
Kingsport
Bristol
Sparta
Mt Airy
Winston-Salem
Johnson City
Morristown
Boone
Elkin
High Point
Greeneville
Knoxville
Spruce Pine
Lenoir
Statesville
Lexington
Maryville
Gatlinburg
Morganton
Hickory
Salisbury
Asheville
Newton
Concord
Albemarle
Cherokee
Lincolnton
Kannapolis
Waynesville
Forest City
Shelby
Franklin
Brevard
Hendersonville
Gastonia
Charlotte
Murphy
Gaffney
Wadesboro
Greenville
Greer
Spartanburg
York
Monroe
Easley
Rock Hill
Cheraw
Clemson
Union
Chester
Lancaster
Belton
Hartsville
Gainesville
Anderson
Laurens
Clinton
Bishopville
Abbeville
Whitmire
Winnsboro
Camden
Greenwood
Columbia
Sumter
Athens
Batesburg
Manning
Edgefield
Aiken
Orangeburg
Williston
Augusta
N. Augusta
Denmark
Bamberg
Milledgeville
Barnwell
Macon
Allendale
Summerville
N. Charleston
Dublin
Walterboro
Charleston
Statesboro
Ridgeland
Beaufort
Cordele
Savannah
Savannah Beach

Clarks Hill Lake
GREAT SMOKY MTS
BLUE RIDGE PKWY
Cumberland Gap Nat'l Hist. Park
Kings Mtn
L. Marion
L. Moultrie

1 2 3 4 5
A B C D E F G H

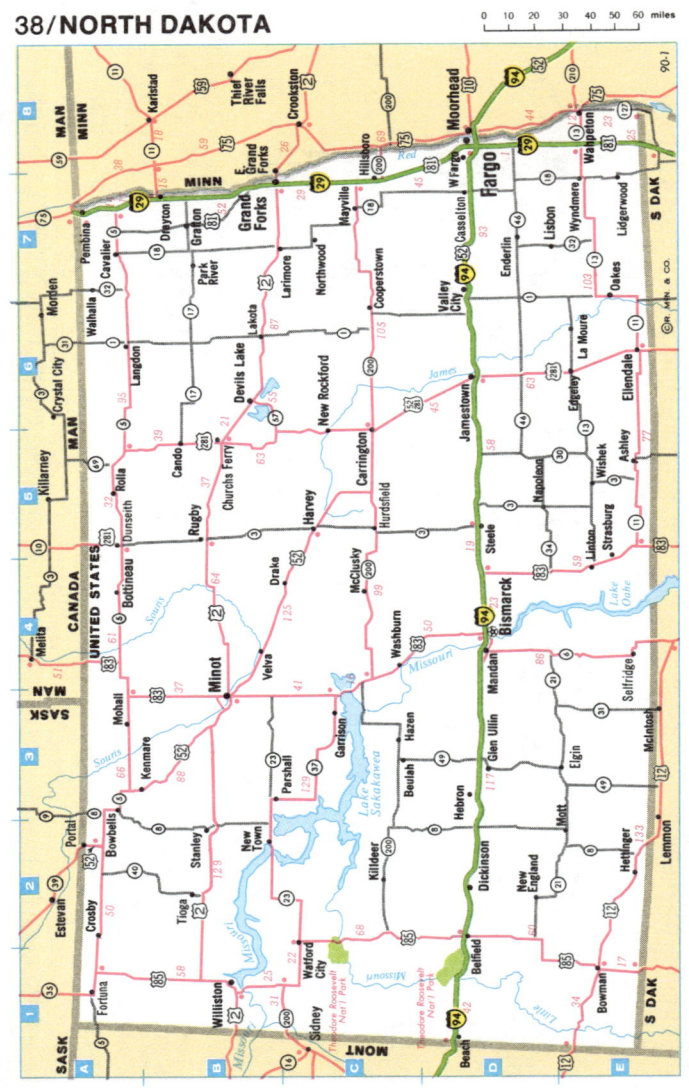

0 10 20 30 40 50 60 70 miles

ARK.

MO

KANS.

COLO.

N. MEX.

TEXAS

Major cities and towns: Ft. Smith, Muskogee, Tulsa, Sapulpa, Okmulgee, Henryetta, Seminole, Shawnee, Norman, Oklahoma City, El Reno, Enid, Guthrie, Chickasha, Lawton, Wichita Falls, Ardmore, Ada, Pauls Valley, Duncan, Marlow, Lindsay, Holdenville, McAlester, Wilburton, Clayton, Antlers, Hugo, Idabel, Atoka, Durant, Denison, Sherman, Gainesville, Denton, Dallas, Ft. Worth, Bowie, Jacksboro, Graham, Seymour, Vernon, Altus, Hobart, Clinton, Weatherford, Elk City, Sayre, Cheyenne, Woodward, Fort Supply, Buffalo, Beaver, Liberal, Guymon, Boise City, Dalhart, Stratford, Dumas, Borger, Pampa, Amarillo, Hereford, Vega, Canadian, Perryton, Shamrock, Memphis, Childress, Paducah, Haskell, Aspermont, Plainview, Lubbock, Post, Tahoka, Brownfield, Littlefield, Vinita, Miami, Bartlesville, Pawhuska, Ponca City, Blackwell, Arkansas City, Coffeyville, Stillwater, Perry, Cushing, Alva, Waynoka, Fairview, Watonga, Kingfisher, Anadarko, Frederick, Snyder, Cordell, Magnum, Hollis, Greenville, McKinney, Terrell, Paris, Sulphur Springs, De Kalb, Poteau, Sallisaw, Talihina, Westville, Tahlequah, Wagoner, Pryor, Claremore

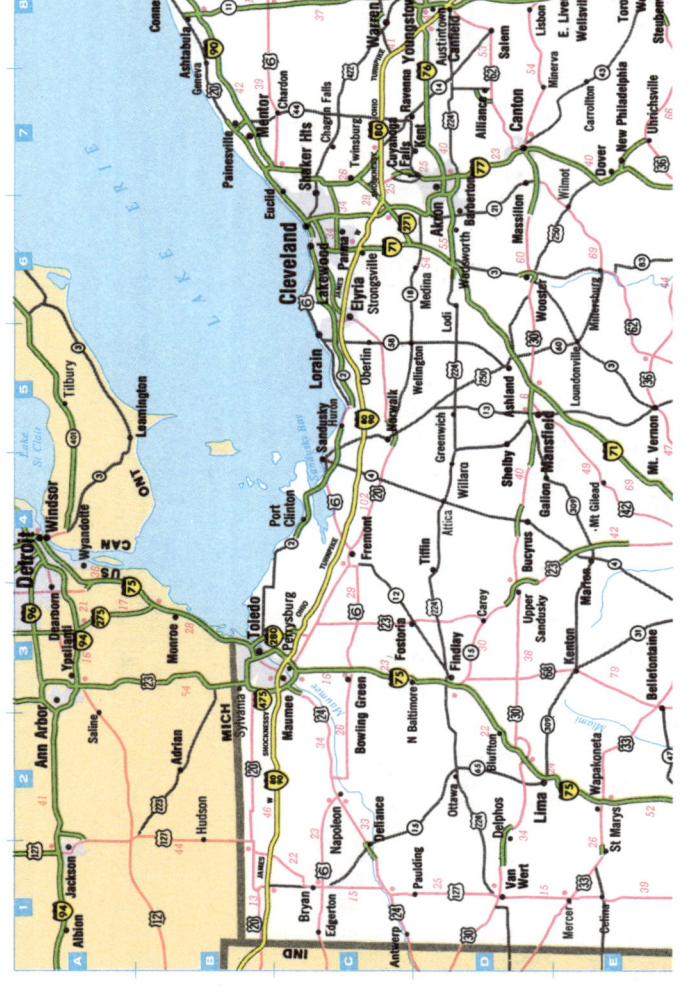

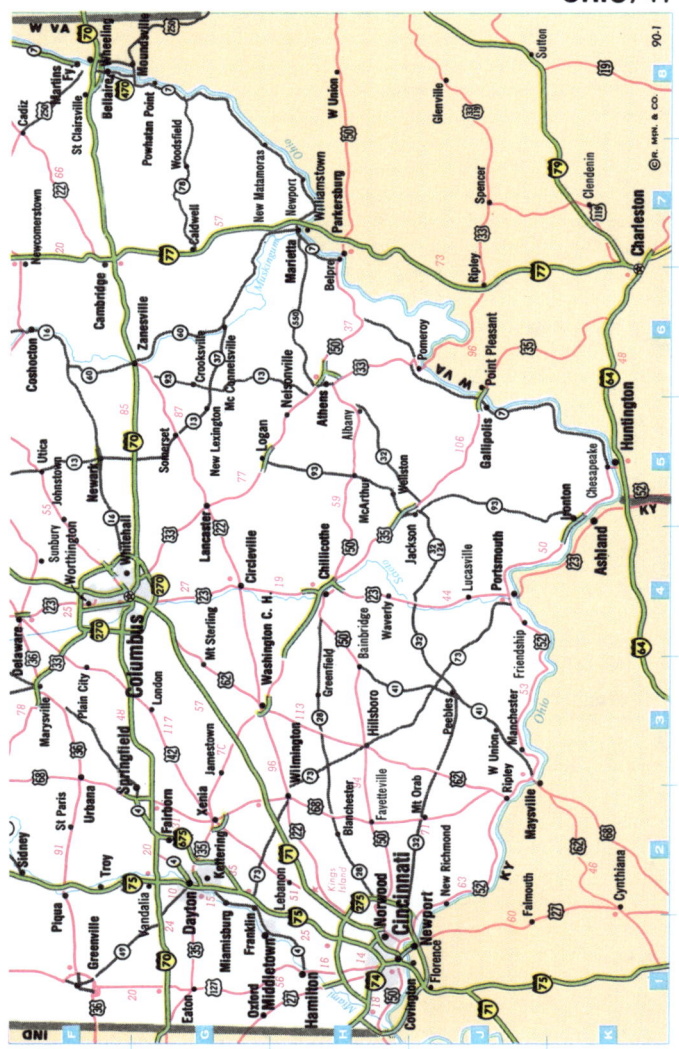

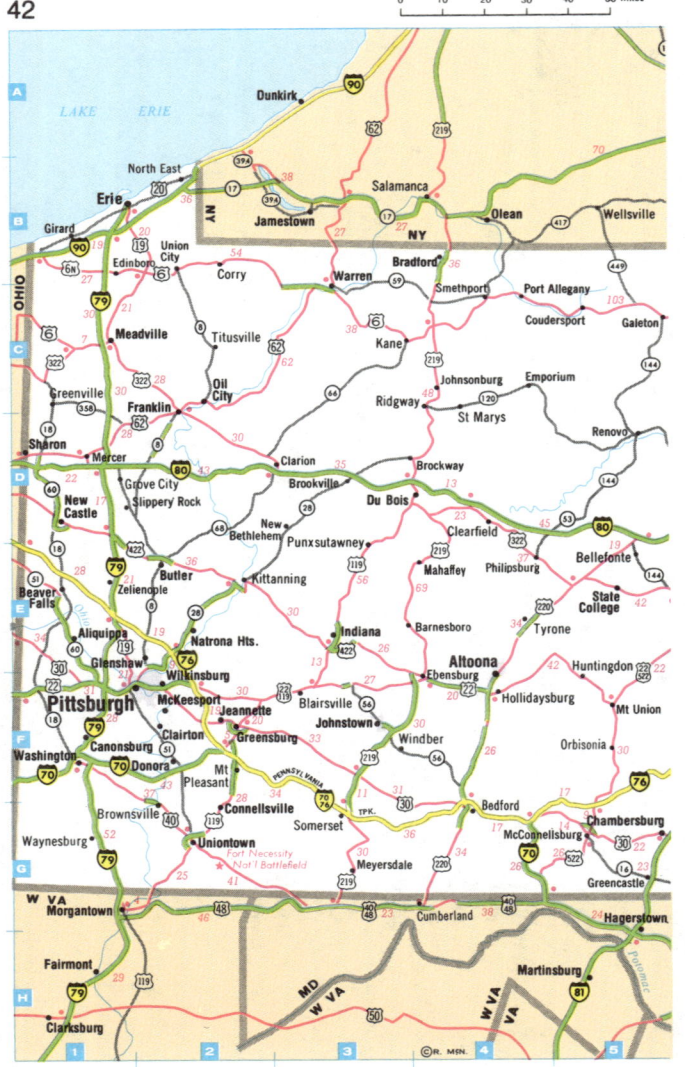

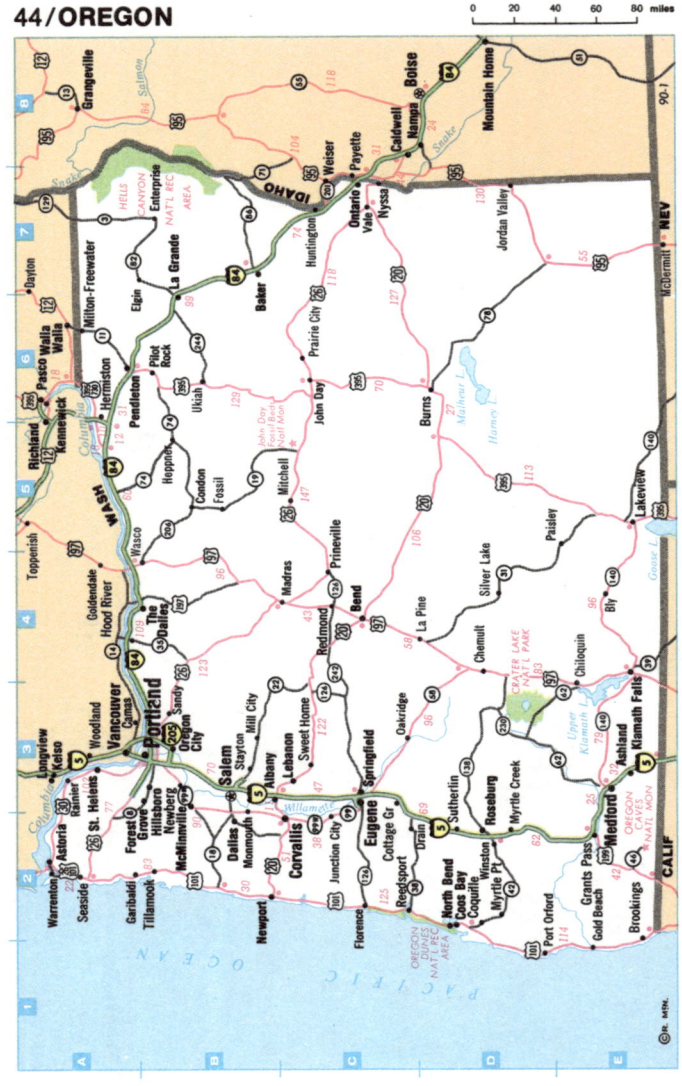

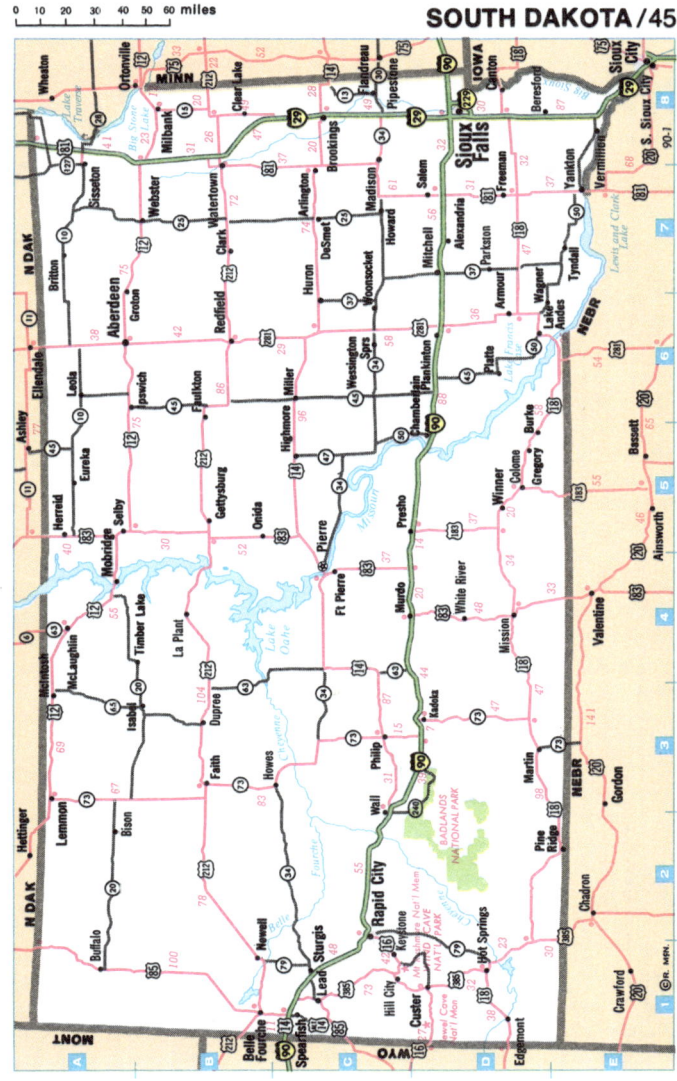

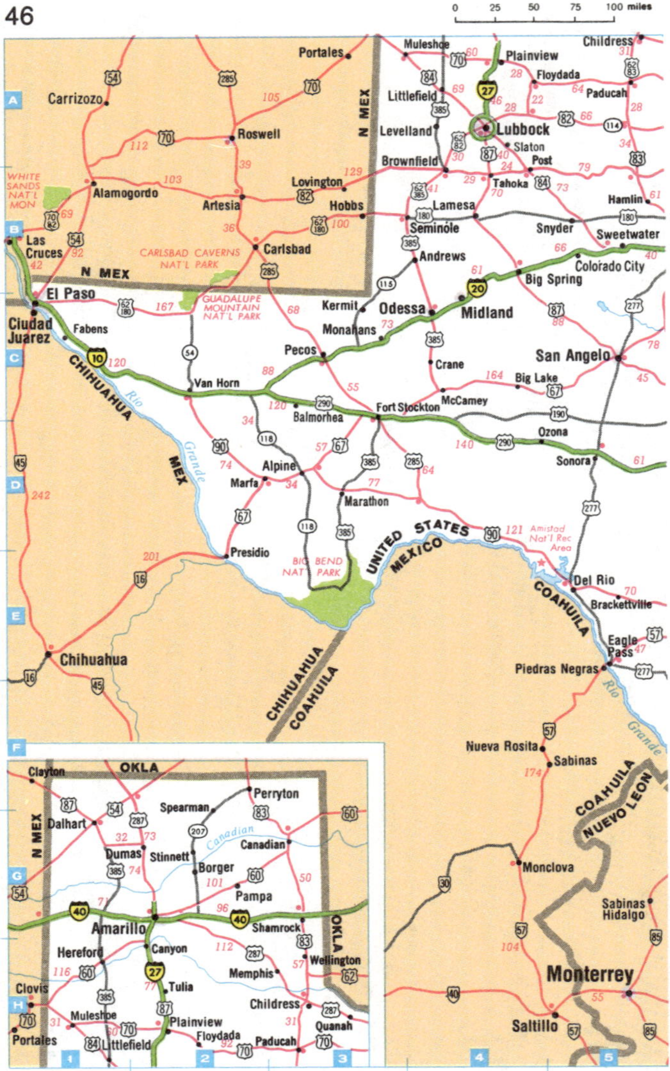
0 25 50 75 100 miles
Portales
Carrizozo
Roswell
Alamogordo
Artesia
Lovington
Hobbs
Las Cruces
Carlsbad
WHITE SANDS NAT'L MON
CARLSBAD CAVERNS NAT'L PARK
N MEX
El Paso
Ciudad Juarez
Fabens
GUADALUPE MOUNTAIN NAT'L PARK
Van Horn
Pecos
Kermit
Odessa
Monahans
Midland
Balmorhea
Fort Stockton
Alpine
Marfa
Marathon
Presidio
BIG BEND NAT'L PARK
Muleshoe
Plainview
Childress
Floydada
Littlefield
Paducah
Levelland
Lubbock
Slaton
Brownfield
Post
Tahoka
Lamesa
Hamlin
Seminole
Snyder
Sweetwater
Andrews
Colorado City
Big Spring
Crane
San Angelo
Big Lake
McCamey
Ozona
Sonora
Amistad Nat'l Rec Area
Del Rio
Brackettville
Eagle Pass
Piedras Negras
CHIHUAHUA
MEX
Rio Grande
UNITED STATES
MEXICO
COAHUILA
Chihuahua
Nueva Rosita
Sabinas
NUEVO LEON
Monclova
Sabinas Hidalgo
Monterrey
Saltillo
Clayton
OKLA
Perryton
Spearman
Dalhart
Canadian
Dumas
Stinnett
Borger
Pampa
Amarillo
Shamrock
Hereford
Canyon
Wellington
Memphis
Tulia
Clovis
Childress
Muleshoe
Plainview
Quanah
Portales
Littlefield
Floydada
Paducah
A B C D E F G H
1 2 3 4 5

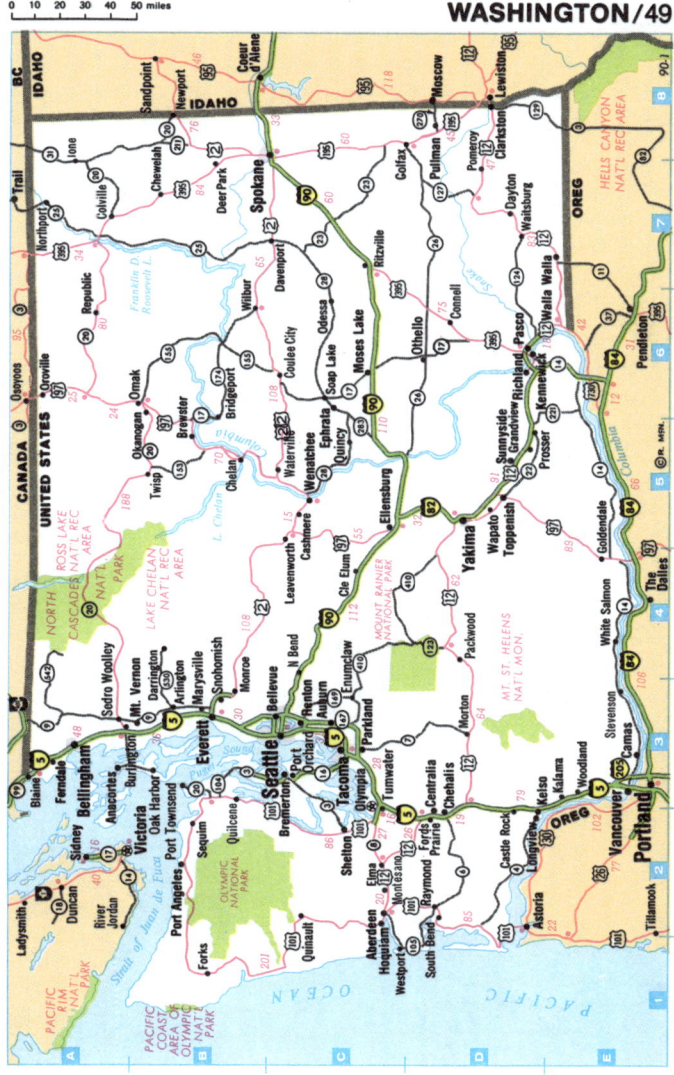

0 10 20 30 40 50 60 miles

ONT
MINN
CAN
US

Rainy Lake
Voyageurs National Park

Thunder Bay

Virginia

LAKE SUPERIOR

Copper Harbor

Isle Royale Nat'l Pk

Houghton
Ontonagon

APOSTLE ISLANDS NATIONAL LAKESHORE

Duluth
Superior

Bayfield
Ashland

Marquette
Ishpeming

Hurley Ironwood
MICH

Iron River

Spooner
Hayward

Park Falls
Eagle River
Woodruff

Iron Mountain
Escanaba

MINN

Rhinelander
Crandon

St Croix Falls
Rice Lake
Ladysmith

Tomahawk

New Richmond
Hudson

Bloomer
Chippewa Falls
Eau Claire

Medford

Merrill
Antigo
Wausau

Marinette
Menominee
Peshtigo
Oconto
Sturgeon Bay

Sister Bay

River Falls
Menomonie
Durand

Marshfield

Shawano

Green Bay
Kewaunee

Red Wing
Whitehall

Neillsville
Stevens Pt.

Clintonville
New London
Waupaca

Neenah
Appleton
Two Rivers
Manitowoc

Black River Falls
Wisconsin Rapids

Wautoma

Winona
Sparta
Tomah
Adams

Oshkosh
Chilton
Sheboygan

La Crosse
Mauston

Wisconsin Dells
Portage

Fond du Lac
Waupun

MINN
IOWA
Decorah

Viroqua

Baraboo
Spring Green
Columbus
Beaver Dam
W Bend
Port Washington

Charles City

Richland Cen
Boscobel

Madison
Monona
Watertown
Menomonee Falls

Milwaukee

Prairie du Chien

Dodgeville
Fort Atkinson
Edgerton
Waukesha
Whitewater

Oelwein

Lancaster
Platteville
Evansville
Janesville
Delavan
Lake Geneva
Burlington

Racine
Kenosha

Waterloo

Dubuque

Monroe
Beloit
ILL

Waukegan

Cedar Rapids
Freeport
Rockford
Elgin

Clinton

Chicago

IOWA
ILL

90-1 ©R. M&N.

0 10 20 30 40 50 miles

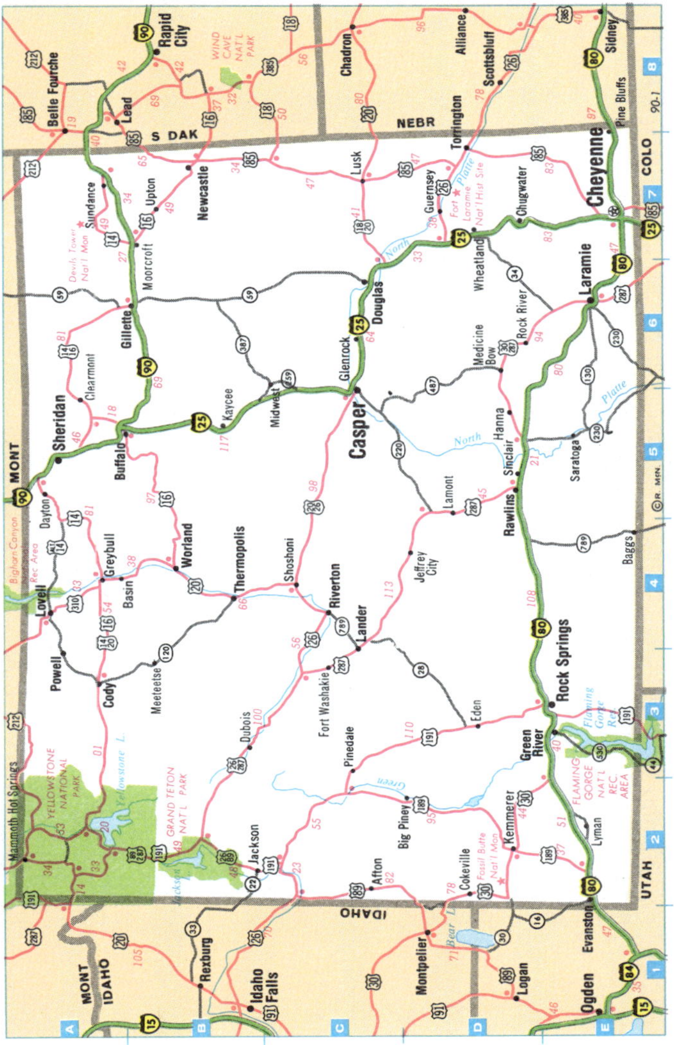
MONT
S DAK
NEBR
COLO
UTAH
IDAHO
MONT
IDAHO
Rapid City
Belle Fourche
Lead
WIND CAVE NAT'L PARK
Chadron
Alliance
Scottsbluff
Torrington
Sidney
Pine Bluffs
Cheyenne
Sundance
Devils Tower Nat'l Mon
Upton
Newcastle
Lusk
Guernsey
Fort Laramie Nat'l Hist Site
Chugwater
Moorcroft
Gillette
Wheatland
Douglas
Glenrock
Medicine Bow
Rock River
Laramie
Sheridan
Clearmont
Buffalo
Kaycee
Midwest
Casper
Hanna
Sinclair
Saratoga
Rawlins
Lamont
Dayton
Bighorn Canyon Nat'l Rec Area
Lowell
Greybull
Basin
Worland
Thermopolis
Shoshoni
Riverton
Lander
Jeffrey City
Baggs
Powell
Cody
Meeteetse
Fort Washakie
Rock Springs
Flaming Gorge Res.
FLAMING GORGE NAT'L REC. AREA
Green River
Eden
Pinedale
Dubois
Mammoth Hot Springs
YELLOWSTONE NATIONAL PARK
Yellowstone L.
GRAND TETON NAT'L PARK
Jackson L.
Jackson
Big Piney
Kemmerer
Lyman
Afton
Cokeville
Fossil Butte Nat'l Mon
Evanston
Bear L.
Montpelier
Rexburg
Idaho Falls
Logan
Ogden
North Platte
Green
©R. McN.
90-1
A B C D E
1 2 3 4 5 6 7 8

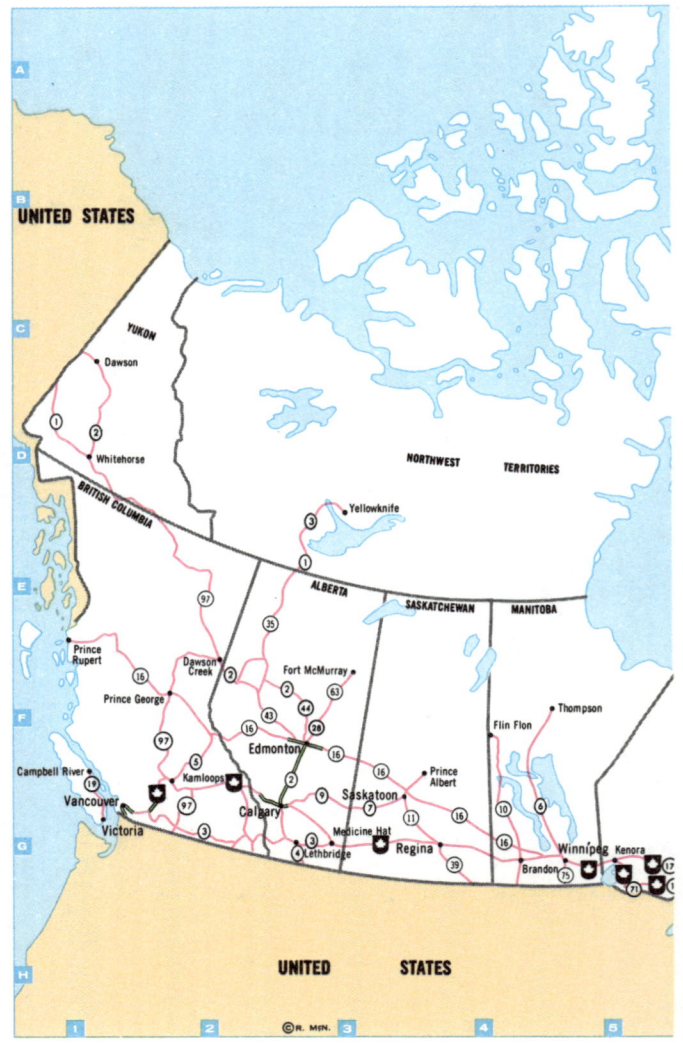

0   100   200   300   400   500 miles

UNITED STATES

YUKON

Dawson

Whitehorse

BRITISH COLUMBIA

NORTHWEST   TERRITORIES

Yellowknife

ALBERTA

SASKATCHEWAN   MANITOBA

Prince
Rupert

Dawson
Creek

Fort McMurray

35

97

16

Prince George

Edmonton

97

Campbell River

Kamloops

Vancouver

Calgary

Victoria

97

Medicine Hat

Lethbridge

Prince
Albert

Saskatoon

Regina

Flin Flon

Thompson

Winnipeg   Kenora

Brandon

UNITED   STATES

CANADA
Principal Highways

Limited Access Freeways
Limited Access Tollways
Other Principal Highways

NEWFOUNDLAND

QUEBEC

St. John's

NEWF.

Corner Brook

ONTARIO

Sept-Iles

P.E.I.

Sydney

Chicoutimi

NEW BRUNS.

Kapuskasing

Riviere-du-Loup
Fredericton

Halifax
NOVA SCOTIA

Timmins

Trois-Rivieres

Saint John

Thunder Bay

North Bay
Sudbury

Ottawa

Sherbrooke

Sault Ste. Marie

Montréal

Toronto
Kitchener
London
Windsor

Hamilton
Niagara Falls

90-1

0 50 100 150 200 250 miles

MEXICO
Principal Highways

Limited Access Tollways

Other Principal Highways

©R. MN. & CO.

UNITED STATES

GUATEMALA

HONDURAS

BELIZE

90-1

Tijuana
Ensenada
Mexicali
Nogales
Hermosillo
Guaymas
Ciudad Juarez
Chihuahua
Hidalgo del Parral
Ciudad Obregón
Culiacan
La Paz
San José del Cabo
Santa Rosalía
Mazatlán
Durango
Torreón
Nueva Rosita
Piedras Negras
Monclova
Saltillo
Monterrey
Nuevo Laredo
Reynosa
Matamoros
Ciudad Victoria
Tampico
San Luis Potosí
Zacatecas
Fresnillo
Aguascalientes
Leon
Irapuato
Querétaro
Guadalajara
Tepic
Puerto Vallarta
Colima
Manzanillo
Morelia
Toluca
Mexico City
Cuernavaca
Taxco
Puebla
Pachuca
Jalapa
Veracruz
Orizaba
Chilpancingo
Acapulco
Oaxaca
Villa Hermosa
Tuxtla Gutierrez
Comitán
Tapachula
Puerto Juárez
Chetumal
Mérida
Campeche

UNITED STATES MILEAGE CHART

From \ To	Albuquerque, N. Mex	Atlanta, Ga.	Birmingham, Ala.	Boston, Mass.	Chicago, Ill.	Cleveland, Ohio	Dallas, Tex.	Denver, Colo.	Detroit, Mich.	Houston, Tex.	Indianapolis, Ind.	Kansas City, Mo.	Los Angeles, Calif.	Mexico City, Mex.	Miami, Fla.	Minneapolis, Minn.	Montreal, Que.	Nashville, Tenn.	New Orleans, La.	New York, N.Y.	Omaha, Nebr.	Philadelphia, Pa.	Phoenix, Ariz.	Portland, Ore.	St. Louis, Mo.	Salt Lake City, Utah	San Francisco, Calif.	Seattle, Wash.	Toronto, Ont.	Washington, D.C.
Albuquerque, N. Mex.	—	1404	1254	2220	1312	1585	644	437	1561	853	1267	777	811	1414	1970	1219	2087	1157	1219	1997	889	1947	458	1312	1042	604	1109	1453	1849	1890
Atlanta, Ga.	1404	—	153	1108	708	732	822	1432	726	789	529	814	2191	1768	663	1118	1196	242	479	854	986	772	1809	2685	541	1878	2496	2734	925	618
Birmingham, Ala.	1254	153	—	1226	657	732	635	1325	754	1068	478	725	2052	1618	754	1092	1235	188	346	978	882	868	1677	2586	512	1791	2365	2540	950	735
Boston, Mass.	2220	1108	1226	—	994	639	1753	1998	699	1830	906	1435	3017	2618	1539	1402	320	1138	1541	213	1435	309	2664	3158	1185	2343	3179	3016	555	448
Chicago, Ill.	1312	708	657	994	—	348	921	1021	279	1091	181	509	2054	2045	1397	405	840	470	919	809	479	785	1742	2117	289	1417	2173	2052	492	709
Cleveland, Ohio	1585	732	732	639	348	—	1189	1362	172	1306	318	791	2382	2251	1252	758	579	534	1138	473	428	432	2032	2432	579	1762	2483	2391	287	360
Dallas, Tex.	644	822	635	1753	921	1189	—	784	1189	243	865	508	1435	1138	1343	936	1715	659	494	1559	662	1443	1002	2043	655	1257	1752	2131	1369	1307
Denver, Colo.	437	1432	1325	1998	1021	1362	784	—	1283	1034	1058	600	1059	1746	2107	920	1301	1183	920	1815	541	1739	813	1261	863	534	1167	1341	1479	1616
Detroit, Mich.	1561	726	754	699	279	172	1189	1283	—	1362	286	784	2311	2288	1385	685	562	543	1070	649	734	609	1970	2384	534	1671	2399	2327	226	516
Houston, Tex.	853	789	1068	1830	1091	1306	243	1034	1362	—	1031	743	1541	979	1190	1246	1825	769	356	1610	864	1511	1164	2243	780	1439	1911	2369	1491	1365
Indianapolis, Ind.	1267	529	478	906	181	318	865	1058	286	1031	—	485	2052	2298	1541	592	892	284	995	713	613	659	1725	2237	246	1566	2289	2245	504	575
Kansas City, Mo.	777	814	725	1435	509	791	508	600	784	743	485	—	1606	2063	1541	466	1063	606	769	1198	201	1170	1235	1820	256	1105	1861	1858	969	1042
Los Angeles, Calif.	811	2191	2052	3017	2054	2382	1435	1059	2311	1541	2052	1606	—	1577	2716	1857	2873	1905	1858	2794	1669	2703	376	962	1836	691	387	1134	2537	2646
Mexico City, Mex.	1414	1768	1618	2618	2045	2251	1138	1746	2288	979	2298	2063	1577	—	1917	1965	1627	1917	2169	2074	1747	1335	1747	2437	1782	2487	2291	2562	2566	2354
Miami, Fla.	1970	663	754	1539	1397	1252	1343	2107	1385	1190	1541	1541	2716	1917	—	1771	1654	910	860	1334	1636	1230	2348	3257	1226	2560	3093	3303	1509	1057
Minneapolis, Minn.	1219	1118	1092	1402	405	758	936	920	685	1246	592	466	1857	1965	1771	—	1163	1073	1301	1217	380	1195	1677	1724	559	1312	1979	1653	897	1090
Montreal, Que.	2087	1196	1235	320	840	579	1715	1301	562	1825	892	1063	2873	1627	1654	1163	—	1074	1591	378	1278	449	2519	2755	1075	2209	2961	2816	337	579
Nashville, Tenn.	1157	242	188	1138	470	534	659	1183	543	769	284	606	1905	1917	910	1073	1074	—	532	900	764	787	1674	2869	321	1703	2325	2442	754	699
New Orleans, La.	1219	479	346	1541	919	1138	494	920	1070	356	995	769	1858	2169	860	1301	1591	532	—	1335	1026	1229	1456	2666	698	1775	2278	2650	1099	1099
New York, N.Y.	1997	854	978	213	809	473	1559	1815	649	1610	713	1198	2794	2074	1334	1217	378	900	1335	—	1252	101	2445	2914	978	2189	2930	2841	469	237
Omaha, Nebr.	889	986	882	1435	479	428	662	541	734	864	613	201	1669	1747	1636	380	1278	764	1026	1252	—	1204	1352	1692	444	936	1691	1692	942	1135
Philadelphia, Pa.	1947	772	868	309	785	432	1443	1739	609	1511	659	1170	2703	1335	1230	1195	449	787	1229	101	1204	—	2445	2859	902	2154	2902	2816	453	143
Phoenix, Ariz.	458	1809	1677	2664	1742	2032	1002	813	1970	1164	1725	1235	376	1747	2348	1677	2519	1674	1456	2445	1352	2445	—	1268	1481	645	762	1465	2183	2300
Portland, Ore.	1312	2685	2586	3158	2117	2432	2043	1261	2384	2243	2237	1820	962	2437	3257	1724	2755	2869	2666	2914	1692	2859	1268	—	2057	763	637	174	2566	2784
St. Louis, Mo.	1042	541	512	1185	289	579	655	863	534	780	246	256	1836	1782	1226	559	1075	321	698	978	444	902	1481	2057	—	1362	2118	2135	739	862
Salt Lake City, Utah	604	1878	1791	2343	1417	1762	1257	534	1671	1439	1566	1105	691	2487	2560	1312	2209	1703	1775	2189	936	2154	645	763	1362	—	752	848	1873	2048
San Francisco, Calif.	1109	2483	2365	3128	2173	2483	1752	1167	2399	1911	2289	1861	387	2291	3093	1979	2961	2325	2278	2930	1691	2902	762	637	2118	752	—	810	2625	2843
Seattle, Wash.	1453	2734	2540	3016	2052	2391	2131	1341	2327	2369	2245	1858	1134	2562	3303	1653	2816	2442	2650	2841	1692	2816	1465	174	2135	848	810	—	2496	2721
Toronto, Ont.	1849	925	950	555	492	287	1369	1479	226	1491	504	969	2537	2566	1509	897	337	754	1134	469	942	453	2183	2566	739	1873	2625	2496	—	456
Washington, D.C.	1890	618	735	448	709	360	1307	1616	516	1365	575	1042	2646	2354	1057	1090	579	699	1099	237	1135	143	2300	2784	862	2048	2843	2721	456	—

Mileages Copyright © 1987 by Rand McNally-TDM, Inc.

ALABAMA

(Map on page 4)
Pop.: 4,093,100
(12-31-86 Estimate)
Area: 50,766 Sq. Mi.
Capital: Montgomery

Albertville ... B-4
Alexander City D-4
Andalusia ... G-3
Anniston C-4
Athens A-3
Atmore G-2
Bay Minette . G-2
Bessemer ... C-3
Birmingham . C-3
Cullman B-3
Decatur A-3
Demopolis .. E-2
Dothan G-5
Enterprise .. G-4
Eufaula F-5
Florala G-4
Florence A-2
Gadsden B-4
Greenville .. F-3
Guntersville . B-3
Homewood .. C-3
Huntsville ... A-3
Jacksonville . C-4
Leeds C-3
Mobile H-1
Montgomery . E-3
Muscle Shoals A-2
Opelika D-5
Prichard G-1
Saraland G-1
Selma E-3
Sylacauga .. B-4
Talladega ... C-4
Tarrant City . C-3
Thomasville . F-2
Troy F-4
Tuscaloosa .. A-2
Tuscubia ... A-2
Tuskegee ... E-4

ALASKA

(Map on page 5)
Pop.: 551,700
(12-31-86 Estimate)
Area: 570,833 Sq. Mi.
Capital: Juneau

Anchorage .. C-3
Barrow A-3
Bethel C-2
Cordova C-3
Fairbanks ... B-3
Juneau C-5
Kenai C-3
Ketchikan ... D-5
Nome B-2
Petersburg .. D-5
Port Heiden .. D-2

Sitka D-5
Spenard C-3
Valdez C-3

ARIZONA

(Map on page 6-7)
Pop.: 3,327,400
(12-31-86 Estimate)
Area: 113,510 Sq. Mi.
Capital: Phoenix

Ajo G-2
Avondale ... F-3
Bisbee H-5
Casa Grande . F-3
Coolidge F-3
Douglas H-5
Flagstaff D-3
Gila Bend ... F-2
Glendale E-3
Globe F-4
Grand Canyon C-3
Lake Havasu
City D-1
Mesa F-3
Morenci F-5
Nogales H-4
Page B-4
Phoenix E-3
Prescott D-3
Safford F-5
Scottsdale ... F-3
Sun City E-3
Tempe F-3
Tucson G-4
Winslow D-4
Yuma F-1

ARKANSAS

(Map on page 8-9)
Pop.: 2,404,800
(12-31-86 Estimate)
Area: 52,082 Sq. Mi.
Capital: Little Rock

Arkadelphia . D-3
Batesville ... B-4
Blytheville .. A-6
Booneville .. B-2
Camden D-3
Clarksville .. B-2
Conway C-3
Crossett E-4
Danville C-2
El Dorado ... E-3
Eudora E-5
Fayetteville . A-1
Forrest City . C-5
Ft. Smith ... B-1
Harrison A-3
Helena C-5
Hope D-2
Hot Sprs.
Nat'l. Pk. .. C-3
Jacksonville . C-4

Jonesboro .. B-5
Lake Village . E-5
Little Rock ... C-4
Magnolia ... E-2
Marianna ... C-5
Marked Tree . B-6
Mena C-1
Morrilton ... B-3
Newport B-5
N. Little Rock C-4
Paragould .. A-6
Pine Bluff ... D-4
Russellville .. B-3
Salem A-4
Springdale .. A-2
Stuttgart C-4
Texarkana .. D-2
Van Buren .. B-1
Warren D-4
W. Memphis . B-6

CALIFORNIA

(Map on page 10-11)
Pop.: 27,080,800
(12-31-86 Estimate)
Area: 156,297 Sq. Mi.
Capital: Sacramento

Anaheim J-5
Atwater E-3
Auburn D-3
Bakersfield .. G-5
Barstow H-6
Berkeley E-2
Blythe J-8
Chula Vista .. K-6
Clovis F-4
Davis D-3
El Cajon K-6
El Centro ... K-7
Eureka B-1
Fairfield D-2
Fremont E-2
Fresno F-4
Glendale H-5
Hollister F-3
Lancaster ... H-5
Long Beach ..J-5
Los Angeles ..J-5
Los Banos .. F-3
Madera F-4
Merced E-3
Modesto E-3
Monterey ... F-2
Napa D-2
Newport
Beach J-5
Novato E-2
Oakland E-2
Oceanside ...J-6
Oroville C-3
Oxnard H-4
Palm Springs .J-6
Palo Alto ... E-2
Paradise C-3
Pasadena ... H-5

Placerville ... D-3
Pomona J-5
Redding B-2
Richmond ... E-2
Riverside J-6
Sacramento . D-3
Salinas F-3
San
Bernardino H-6
San Diego ... K-6
San Francisco E-2
San Jose ... E-2
San Luis
Obispo G-3
San Mateo .. E-2
Santa Ana ...J-5
Santa Barbara H-4
Santa Cruz .. F-2
Santa Monica .J-5
Santa Rosa .. D-2
South Lake
Tahoe D-4
Stockton E-3
Susanville ... B-3
Turlock E-3
Ukiah D-1
Vallejo E-2
Ventura H-4
Visalia F-4
Watsonville .. F-2
Woodland ... D-3
Yreka A-2
Yuba City ... D-3

COLORADO

(Map on page 14)
Pop.: 3,300,100
(12-31-86 Estimate)
Area: 103,598 Sq. Mi.
Capital: Denver

Alamosa E-4
Aspen C-3
Aurora B-5
Boulder B-5
Brighton B-5
Canon City .. D-5
Cimarron ... D-3
Colorado
Springs C-5
Cortez E-2
Craig A-3
Delta C-2
Denver B-5
Durango E-2
Englewood .. B-5
Ft. Collins ... A-5
Ft. Morgan .. B-6
Glenwood
Springs B-3
Grand
Junction ... C-2
Greeley A-5
Gunnison ... C-3
La Junta D-6
Lakewood ... B-5

60

MISSISSIPPI

(Map on pages 8-9)
Pop.: 2,668,400
(12-31-86 Estimate)
Area: 47,234 Sq. Mi.
Capital: Jackson

Aberdeen	D-8
Biloxi	H-8
Booneville	C-8
Brookhaven	G-6
Canton	F-6
Clarksdale	D-6
Cleveland	D-5
Columbia	G-6
Columbus	D-8
Corinth	C-8
Greenville	E-5
Greenwood	D-6
Grenada	D-6
Gulfport	H-7
Hattiesburg	G-7
Holly Sprs.	C-7
Indianola	D-5
Jackson	F-6
Kosciusko	E-7
Laurel	G-7
Louisville	E-7
McComb	G-6
Mendenhall	F-6
Meridian	F-8
Moss Pt.	H-8
Natchez	G-5
New Albany	C-7
Oxford	C-7
Pascagoula	H-8
Philadelphia	E-7
Quitman	F-8
Senatobia	C-6
Starkville	D-7
Tupelo	C-8
Vicksburg	F-5
Winona	D-6
Woodville	H-5
Yazoo City	E-6

MISSOURI

(Map on page 29)
Pop.: 5,149,300
(12-31-86 Estimate)
Area: 68,945 Sq. Mi.
Capital: Jefferson City

Bethany	A-3
Bismarck	D-6
Boonville	B-4
Cape Girardeau	D-7
Carthage	D-3
Chillicothe	B-4
Columbia	B-5
Eldon	C-4
Excelsior Springs	B-3
Festus	C-6
Fulton	C-5
Hannibal	B-5
Independence	B-3
Jefferson City	C-5
Joplin	D-3
Kansas City	B-3
Kennett	E-6
Kirksville	A-4
Lees Summit	B-3
Marshall	B-4
Mexico	B-5
Milan	A-4
Moberly	B-4
Mound City	A-2
Nevada	D-3
New Madrid	E-7
Palmyra	B-5
Piedmont	D-6
Poplar Bluff	E-6
Rolla	C-5
St. Charles	C-6
St. Joseph	B-3
St. Louis	C-6
Salem	D-5
Sedalia	C-4
Sikeston	D-7
Springfield	D-4
Warrensburg	C-3
W. Plains	E-5

MONTANA

(Map on page 30)
Pop.: 841,700
(12-31-86 Estimate)
Area: 145,388 Sq. Mi.
Capital: Helena

Anaconda	D-3
Billings	D-5
Bozeman	D-4
Browning	A-3
Butte	D-3
Columbia Falls	A-2
Deer Lodge	C-3
Dillon	D-3
Ekalaka	D-8
Eureka	A-1
Glasgow	B-7
Glendive	C-8
Great Falls	B-4
Hardin	D-6
Harlem	A-5
Havre	A-5
Helena	C-3
Kalispell	B-2
Lewistown	C-5
Libby	A-1
Livingston	D-4
Miles City	C-7
Missoula	C-2
Phillipsburg	C-2
Roundup	C-5
Shelby	A-3
Superior	C-1
Thompson Falls	B-1
Whitefish	A-2
Wolf Pt.	B-7

NEBRASKA

(Map on page 31)
Pop.: 1,624,600
(12-31-86 Estimate)
Area: 76,639 Sq. Mi.
Capital: Lincoln

Ainsworth	B-4
Alliance	B-2
Alma	E-5
Auburn	D-8
Bayard	C-1
Beatrice	D-7
Blair	C-8
Bridgeport	C-1
Broken Bow	C-4
Crawford	A-1
Fairbury	D-7
Falls City	D-8
Fremont	C-7
Gering	B-1
Grand Island	D-6
Hastings	D-6
Holdrege	D-5
Kimball	C-1
Lincoln	D-7
Loup City	C-5
McCook	D-4
Nebraska City	D-8
Neligh	B-6
Norfolk	B-6
North Platte	C-4
Ogallala	C-3
Omaha	C-8
O'Neill	B-5
Oshkosh	C-2
Plattsmouth	C-8
Red Cloud	D-6
Rushville	A-2
Scottsbluff	B-1
Seward	D-7
Sidney	C-2
Syracuse	D-8
Valentine	A-4
Wayne	B-7
York	D-6

NEVADA

(Map on page 10-11)
Pop.: 963,900
(12-31-86 Estimate)
Area: 109,895 Sq. Mi.
Capital: Carson City

Austin	C-6
Babbitt	D-5
Battle Mtn.	B-6
Boulder City	G-8
Carlin	B-7
Carson City	D-4
Elko	B-7
Ely	C-8
Empire	B-4
Eureka	C-7
Fallon	C-5
Hawthorne	D-5
Henderson	G-8
Indian Sprs.	F-7
Las Vegas	G-8
Lovelock	C-5
N. Las Vegas	F-8
Overton	F-8
Reno	C-4
Sparks	C-4
Tonopah	E-6
Warm Sprs.	D-7
Wells	B-7
Winnemucca	B-5
Yerington	D-4

NEW HAMPSHIRE

(Map on page 32)
Pop.: 1,025,100
(12-31-86 Estimate)
Area: 8,992 Sq. Mi.
Capital: Concord

Ashland	E-4
Berlin	C-4
Bristol	E-4
Center Ossipee	E-5
Claremont	F-3
Colebrook	B-4
Concord	F-4
Conway	D-5
Derry	G-4
Dover	F-5
Franklin	E-4
Hampton	G-5
Keene	G-3
Laconia	E-4
Lebanon	E-3
Littleton	C-3
Manchester	G-4
Nashua	G-4
N. Woodstock	D-4
Peterborough	G-3
Portsmouth	F-5
Rochester	F-5
Salem	G-4
Winchester	G-3
Woodsville	D-4

NEW JERSEY

(Map on page 33)
Pop.: 7,687,300
(12-31-86 Estimate)
Area: 7,468 Sq. Mi.
Capital: Trenton

Asbury Park	D-5
Atlantic City	G-4
Bayonne	C-4
Bloomfield	B-4
Bridgeton	G-2
Burlington	E-3
Camden	E-2
Clifton	B-4

Aberdeen ... A-6	Ripley F-2	San Marcos .. D-7	Manchester . E-1
Arlington C-8	Rogersville .. E-9	Sherman A-8	Middlebury .. D-1
Armour D-6	Shelbyville .. G-5	Snyder B-5	Montpelier ... D-2
Belle Fourche B-1	Soddy-Daisy . G-7	Sulphur Springs	Newport B-3
Brookings ... C-8	Tullahoma ... G-5	.... B-9	Northfield ... D-2
Custer D-1	Union City .. E-2	Sweetwater .. B-5	Norton B-3
Faith B-3	Waverly F-3	Temple C-7	Poultney E-1
Gettysburg .. B-5		Texarkana .. A-10	Rutland E-1
Hot Springs . D-1		Texas City .. E-9	St. Albans ... B-1
Lemmon A-3		Tyler B-9	St. Johnsbury C-3
Madison C-8	**TEXAS**	Vernon A-6	Springfield .. F-2
Mitchell D-7	*(Map on page 46-47)*	Victoria E-8	Swanton B-1
Mobridge ... A-4	Pop.: 16,738,100	Waco C-8	Waterbury ... C-2
Philip C-3	(12-31-86 Estimate)	Waxahachie . B-8	Winooski C-1
Pierre C-4	Area: 262,015 Sq. Mi.	Wichita Falls . A-7	Woodstock .. E-2
Plankinton .. D-6	Capital: Austin		
Presho C-5			
Rapid City .. C-2	Abilene B-6		
Redfield B-6	Amarillo G-2	**UTAH**	**VIRGINIA**
Sioux Falls .. D-8	Arlington B-8	*(Map on page 48)*	*(Map on page 24-25)*
Sisseton A-8	Austin D-7	Pop.: 1,704,200	Pop.: 5,845,100
Spearfish ... C-1	Baytown D-9	(12-31-86 Estimate)	(12-31-86 Estimate)
Sturgis C-1	Beaumont .. D-10	Area: 82,076 Sq. Mi.	Area: 39,700 Sq. Mi.
Watertown .. B-8	Big Spring .. B-4	Capital: Salt Lake City	Capital: Richmond
Yankton E-7	Borger G-2		
	Brownfield .. B-4	American	Alexandria .. D-8
	Brownsville . H-7	Fork C-3	Arlington D-8
	Brownwood .. C-6	Bountiful C-3	Big Stone Gap F-2
TENNESSEE	Bryan D-8	Brigham City B-3	Bowling
(Map on page 22-23)	Corpus Christi F-7	Cedar City .. G-2	Green E-8
Pop.: 4,852,500	Corsicana ... B-8	Clearfield ... B-3	Bristol G-2
(12-31-86 Estimate)	Dallas B-8	Green River .. E-4	Buena Vista . E-6
Area: 41,154 Sq. Mi.	Del Rio E-5	Kearns C-3	Charlottesville E-7
Capital: Nashville	Denton B-8	Layton C-3	Chesapeake .. G-9
	Eagle Pass .. E-5	Loa F-3	Colonial Hts.. F-8
Athens G-7	El Paso C-1	Logan B-3	Covington ... E-5
Bolivar G-2	Ft. Worth ... B-7	Moab F-5	Danville G-6
Bristol E-10	Freeport E-9	Murray C-3	Emporia G-8
Chattanooga G-7	Gainesville .. A-7	Ogden B-3	Franklin G-8
Clarksville .. E-4	Galveston ... E-9	Orem C-3	Fredericksburg
Cleveland ... G-7	Harlingen ... H-7	Price D-4	.... D-8
Columbia F-4	Houston D-9	Provo D-3	Front Royal .. D-7
Cookeville .. F-6	Huntsville .. D-9	Richfield E-3	Hampton F-9
Crossville ... F-7	Jacksonville . C-9	St. George .. G-1	Harrisonburg D-6
Dyersburg .. F-2	Kermit C-3	Salt Lake	Lynchburg ... F-6
Elizabethton E-10	Kerrville D-6	City C-3	Martinsville .. G-5
Fayetteville . G-5	Kingsville ... F-7	Smithfield ... B-3	New Market .. D-6
Greeneville .. F-9	Lake Jackson E-9	Spanish Fork D-3	Newport News F-9
Harriman F-7	Lamesa B-4	Tremonton .. B-2	Norfolk G-9
Henderson .. G-2	Laredo F-6	Vernal C-5	Onancock .. E-10
Hohenwald .. G-4	Longview B-9	Vernon D-2	Orange E-7
Humbolt F-2	Lubbock A-4	Wendover ... C-1	Petersburg .. F-8
Jackson F-2	Lufkin C-9		Portsmouth . G-9
Johnson City E-10	McAllen G-7		Pulaski F-4
Kingsport ... E-9	Marshall B-9	**VERMONT**	Radford F-4
Knoxville F-8	Midland C-4	*(Map on page 32)*	Reedville E-9
Lafayette E-5	Nacogdoches C-9	Pop.: 544,000	Richmond ... F-8
Lawrenceburg	Odessa C-4	(12-31-86 Estimate)	Roanoke F-5
.... G-4	Orange D-10	Area: 9,273 Sq. Mi.	Staunton E-6
Lebanon F-5	Palestine ... C-9	Capital: Montpelier	Suffolk G-9
McMinnville . F-6	Paris A-9		Tappahannock
Maryville F-8	Pecos C-3	Barre D-2	.... E-8
Memphis G-1	Perryton F-2	Bennington .. G-1	Tazewell F-3
Millington ... G-1	Plainview A-4	Bradford D-3	Virginia Beach F-9
Morristown .. F-9	Port Arthur . D-10	Brattleboro .. G-2	Warrenton ... D-7
Murfreesboro F-5	Presidio E-2	Burlington ... C-1	Waynesboro . E-6
Nashville F-5	Raymondville G-7	Fair Haven ... E-1	Williamsburg F-9
Oak Ridge ... F-7	San Angelo .. C-5	Island Pond .. B-3	Winchester .. C-7
Paris E-3	San Antonio . E-7	Lyndonville .. C-3	Wytheville ... F-4

64

WASHINGTON
(Map on page 49)
Pop.: 4,479,300
(12-31-86 Estimate)
Area: 66,512 Sq. Mi.
Capital: Olympia

Aberdeen C-2
Auburn C-3
Bellevue C-3
Bellingham .. A-3
Blaine A-3
Bremerton ... C-3
Camas E-3
Cheney C-7
Clarkston ... D-8
Colville A-7
Coulee Dam .. B-6
Ellensburg .. C-5
Ephrata C-6
Everett B-3
Hoquiam C-2
Kennewick ... D-6
Longview D-2
Moses Lake .. C-6
Mt. Vernon .. B-3
Olympia C-2
Omak B-6
Oroville A-6
Parkland C-3
Pasco D-6
Port Angeles . B-2
Pullman D-8
Renton C-3
Richland D-6
Seattle C-3
Sedro
  Woolley ... A-3
Spokane C-8
Sunnyside ... D-5
Tacoma C-3
Toppenish ... D-5
Vancouver ... E-3
Walla Walla . E-7
Wenatchee ... C-6
White Salmon E-4
Yakima D-5

WEST VIRGINIA
(Map on page 24-25)
Pop.: 1,951,100
(12-31-86 Estimate)
Area: 24,124 Sq. Mi.
Capital: Charleston

Beckley E-4
Bluefield ... F-3
Charleston .. D-3
Clarksburg .. C-5
Elkins D-5
Fairmont C-5
Franklin D-6
Huntington .. D-2
Logan E-3
Madison E-3
Marlinton ... E-5
Martinsburg . C-7

Morgantown . C-5
New
  Martinsville C-4
Parkersburg . C-3
Petersburg .. D-6
Pt. Pleasant . D-3
Princeton ... F-4
St. Albans .. D-3
Spencer D-3
Summersville D-4
Weirton B-4
Weston C-4
Wheeling B-4
White Sulphur
  Springs ... E-4

WISCONSIN
(Map on page 50)
Pop.: 4,834,600
(12-31-86 Estimate)
Area: 54,424 Sq. Mi.
Capital: Madison

Appleton E-4
Ashland C-2
Baraboo F-3
Beaver Dam .. G-4
Beloit G-4
Chippewa
  Falls E-2
Eagle River . D-3
Eau Claire .. E-2
Fond Du Lac . F-4
Green Bay ... E-4
Hayward C-2
Janesville .. G-4
Kenosha G-5
La Crosse ... F-2
Lake Geneva . G-4
Madison G-3
Manitowoc ... F-5
Marinette ... D-5
Marshfield .. E-3
Menomonee
  Falls G-4
Merrill D-3
Milwaukee ... G-5
Neenah F-4
Oshkosh F-4
Prairie du
  Chien G-2
Racine G-5
Rhinelander . D-3
Rice Lake ... D-2
Shawano E-4
Sheboygan ... F-5
Stevens Pt. . E-3
Sturgeon
  Bay E-5
Superior C-1
Two Rivers .. F-5
Waukesha G-4
Wausau E-3
Wisconsin
  Dells F-3
Wisconsin
  Rapids E-3

WYOMING
(Map on page 51)
Pop.: 512,300
(12-31-86 Estimate)
Area: 96,988 Sq. Mi.
Capital: Cheyenne

Buffalo B-5
Casper C-6
Cheyenne E-7
Cody A-3
Douglas C-6
Evanston E-2
Gillette B-6
Green River . E-3
Jackson B-2
Lander C-4
Laramie E-6
Lovell A-4
Lusk C-7
Mammoth Hot
  Springs ... A-2
Newcastle ... B-7
Pinedale C-3
Powell A-3
Rawlins D-5
Riverton C-4
Rock Sprs. .. E-3
Sheridan A-5
Sundance A-7
Thermopolis . B-4
Torrington .. D-7
Worland B-4

CANADA
(Map on page 52-53)
Pop.: 24,343,181
(1981 Census)
Area:3,851,809
  Sq.Mi.
Capital: Ottawa

Brandon G-4
Calgary G-3
Campbell
  River F-1
Chicoutimi .. G-8
Corner Brook F-10
Dawson C-1
Dawson Creek F-2
Edmonton F-3
Flin Flon ... F-4
Fort McMurray F-3
Fredericton . G-9
Halifax G-9
Hamilton H-7
Kamloops G-2
Kapuskasing . G-7
Kenora G-5
Kitchener ... H-7
Lethbridge .. G-3
London H-7
Medicine Hat G-3
Montréal G-8
Niagara Falls H-7
North Bay ... G-7
Ottawa G-8
Prince Albert F-4

Prince George F-2
Prince Rupert E-1
Quebéc G-8
Regina G-4
Rivière-du-Loup
  .... G-8
Saint John .. G-9
St. John's .. E-10
Saskatoon ... G-3
Sault Ste.
  Marie H-7
Sept-Iles ... F-8
Sherbrooke .. G-8
Sudbury G-7
Sydney F-10
Thompson F-4
Thunder Bay . G-6
Toronto H-7
Trois-Rivières G-8
Vancouver ... G-1
Victoria G-1
Whitehorse .. D-1
Windsor H-7
Winnipeg G-5
Yellowknife . D-3

MEXICO
(Map on page 54)
Pop.: 67,395,826
(1980 Census)
Area:761,604 Sq.Mi.
Capital: Mexico City

Acapulco E-5
Chihuahua ... B-3
Ciudad Juarez A-3
Ciudad
  Obregon ... B-3
Ciudad
  Victoria .. C-5
Colima D-4
Culiacan C-3
Durango C-4
Fresnillo ... C-4
Guadalajara . D-4
Hermosillo .. B-2
La Paz C-2
Matamoros ... C-6
Merida D-7
Mexicali A-1
Mexico D-5
Monterrey ... C-5
Morelia D-5
Nuevo Laredo B-5
Oaxaca E-6
Piedras
  Negras B-5
Puebla D-5
Reynosa B-5
Saltillo C-5
San Luis
  Potosi C-5
Tampico C-5
Tijuana A-1
Toluca D-5
Torreon C-4
Veracruz D-6
Villa Hermosa E-7

Rand McNally Pocket World Atlas

Contents

Map Legend

Urban Area (area of continuous industrial, commercial, and residential development)

The size of type indicates the relative economic and political importance of the locality

Écommoy	Lisieux	**Rouen**
Trouville	**Orléans**	**PARIS**

Capitals of Political Units

BUDAPEST   Independent Nation

Cayenne   Dependency (Colony, protectorate, etc.)

Lasa   State, Province, etc.

Alternate Names

MOSKVA
'MOSCOW'   English or second official language names are shown in reduced size lettering

Volgograd
(Stalingrad)   Historical or other alternates in the local language are shown in parentheses

Political Boundaries

International (First-order political unit)

— ·· — ·· —   Demarcated and Undemarcated

— — —   Indefinite or Undefined

— - - - - - -   Demarcation Line (used in Korea)

Internal

▬▬▬▬   State, Province, etc. (Second-order political unit)

MURCIA   Historical Region (No boundaries indicated)

Transportation

———   Primary Road

———   Secondary Road

Robinson Projection

Miller Oblated Stereographic Projection

ATLANTIC OCEAN

NORTH SEA

ATLANTIC OCEAN

English Channel
La Manche

Conic Projection, Two Standard Parallels

Kilometres 0 50 100 150 Km.
Miles 0 50 100 150 Mi.

1 : 7 500 000

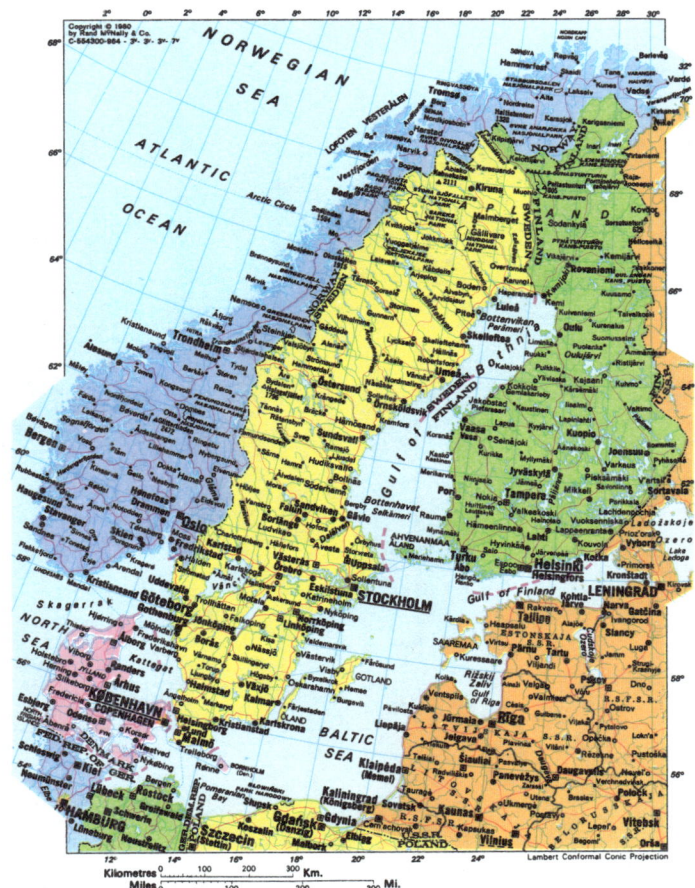

8

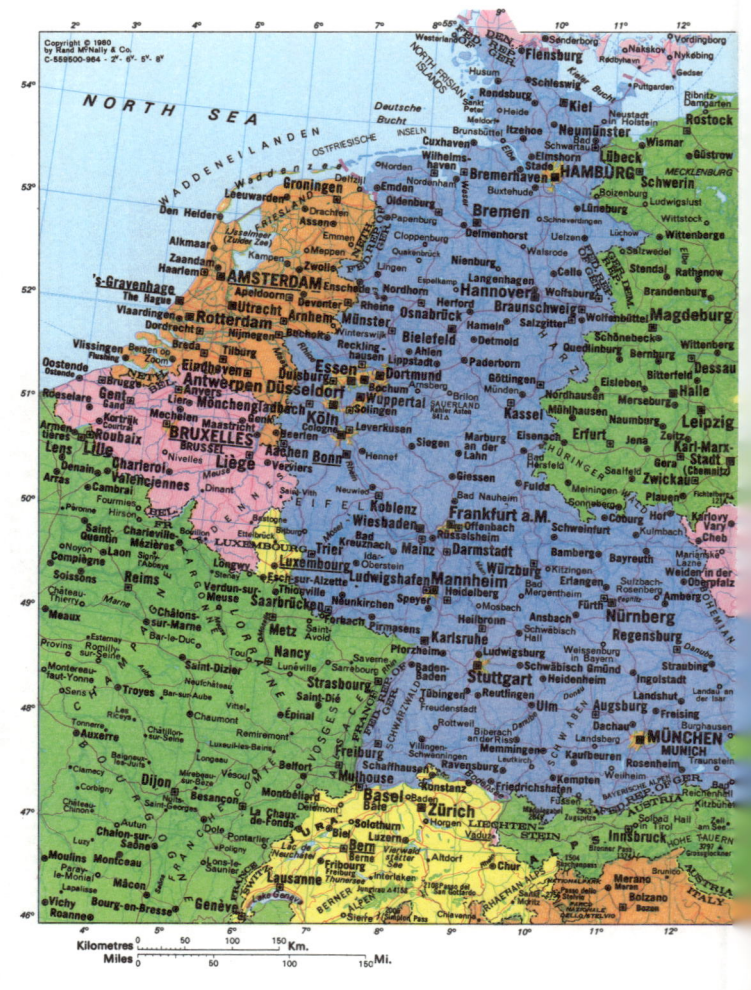

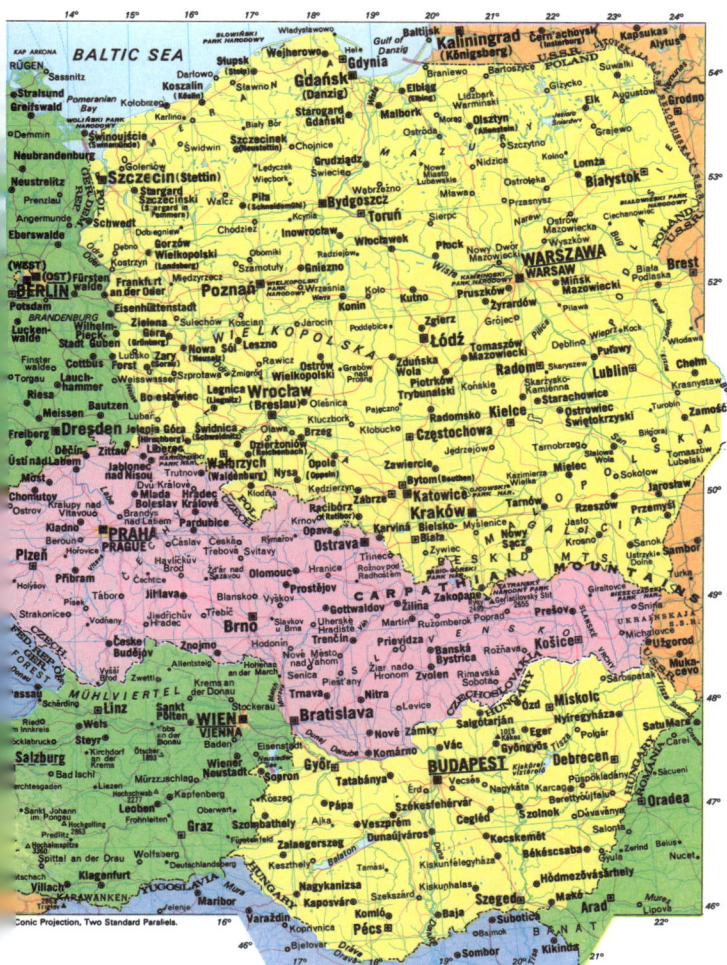

Conic Projection, Two Standard Parallels.

Köln
Cologne
Leverkusen
Frankenberg
Eisenach
Erfurt
Jena
Gera
Karl-Marx-
Stadt Chemnitz
Děčín
Ústí nad Labem

Mechelen
Gent
Siegen
Marburg
an der Lahn
THÜRINGER
WALD
Zwickau
Most
Chomutov
Kralupy
nad Vltavou

Maastricht
Aachen
Bonn
Hennef
Giessen
Fulda
Meiningen
Saalfeld
Plauen
Cheb
Karlovy
Vary
Kladno
PRAHA
PRAGUE

Charleroi
EIFEL
Koblenz
Bad
Nauheim
Coburg
Kulmbach
Bayreuth
Plzeň
Příbram

Dinant
Frankfurt a. M.
Wiesbaden
Mainz
Rüsselsheim
Offenbach
Darmstadt
Bamberg
Weiden in
der Oberpfalz
BOHEMIAN FOREST
Česká
Budějovice

LUXEM-
BOURG
Trier
Luxembourg
Kaiserslautern
Kreuznach
Speyer
Weinheim
Heidelberg
Würzburg
Erlangen
Nürnberg
Amberg
Sulzbach-Rosenberg
Straubing
Linz

Esch-sur-
Alzette
Thionville
Neunkirchen
Pirmasens
Heilbronn
Schwäbisch-
Hall
Fürth
Regensburg
Passau
Schärding

Verdun
Metz
Saarbrücken
Karlsruhe
Pforzheim
Ludwigsburg
Schwäbisch
Gmünd
Ingolstadt
Landshut
Landau an
der Isar

Nancy
Strasbourg
Baden-Baden
Stuttgart
Göppingen
Augsburg
Freising
München
MUNICH
Salzburg

Saint-Dié
Colmar
Offenburg
Freudenstadt
Reutlingen
Ulm
Dachau
Burghausen
AUSTRIA

Épinal
Freiburg
Singen
Memmingen
Ravensburg
Kaufbeuren
Rosenheim
Salzburg
Kirchdorf an
der Krems

Mulhouse
Schaffhausen
Konstanz
Friedrichshafen
Kempten
BAYERISCHE
ALPEN
Kitzbühel
Zell am
See
HOHE TAUERN

Belfort
Basel
Baden
Zürich
Sankt
Gallen
Innsbruck
Spittal an
der Drau

Montbéliard
Solothurn
Luzern
Altdorf
Chur
TIROL

Besançon
Biel
Bern Berne
Interlaken
Vaduz
Merano
Bolzano
DOLOMITI
Udine
Gorizia

La Chaux-
de-Fonds
Fribourg
Freiburg
BERNER ALPEN
Brig
Bozen
Villach

Dijon
Lausanne
Sierre
Brienz
Bellinzona
Trento
Vittorio
Veneto
Pordenone
Treviso
Trieste

Mâcon
Genève
Martigny
Mont-Blanc
Lugano
Lecco
Clusone
Riva
Bassano
del Grappa
Verona
Vicenza
Venezia
Venice
Gulf
of
Venice

Bourg-
en-Bresse
Annecy
Verbania
Varese
Como
Bergamo
Brescia
Padova
Rovigo
ADRIATIC
SEA

Lyon
Villeurbanne
Aix-les-
Bains
Biella
Gallarate
Monza
MILANO
MILAN
Crema
Cremona
Mantova
Ferrara
Bologna

Vienne
Chambéry
Aosta
Novara
Vercelli
Pavia
Piacenza
Fidenza
Modena
Comacchio

Grenoble
Saint-Jean-
de-Maurienne
Rivoli
TORINO
Turin
Casale
Monferrato
Tortona
Parma
Reggio
nell'Emilia

Romans
Valence
Briançon
Pinerolo
Carmagnola
Asti
Alessandria
Novi Ligure
Fidenza
Bondeno
Faenza
Ravenna

Montélimar
Gap
Cuneo
Fossano
GENOVA
Genoa
Savona
La Spezia
Carrara
Pistoia
Bologna
SAN
MARINO
Rimini
Pesaro

Carpentras
Digne
Imperia
San Remo
Golfo di
Genova
Viareggio
Pisa
Empoli
FIRENZE
Florence
Arezzo
Senigallia
Ancona

Avignon
Nice
MONACO
Cannes
Livorno
Leghorn
Siena
Perugia
Macerata

Aix-en-
Provence
Grasse
Fréjus
CÔTE D'AZUR
LIGURIAN
SEA
Cecina
Assisi
Foligno
Spoleto

Marseille
Toulon
Hyères
La Seyne
CAP CORSE
Piombino
ISOLA
D'ELBA
Orvieto
Narni
Rieti

MEDITERRANEAN
SEA
Copyright © 1980
by Rand McNally & Co.
C-559495-964-3¾-3½-3½-8¾
CORSE
CORSICA
Bastia
Calvi
Porto Santo
Stefano
Orbetello
Viterbo

Copyright © 1980
by Rand McNally & Co.
C-559900-984 · 3° · 4° · 5° · 7°

Conic Projection, Two Standard Parallels

Kilometres 0 — 50 — 100 — 150
Miles 0 — 50 — 100 — 150 Mi.

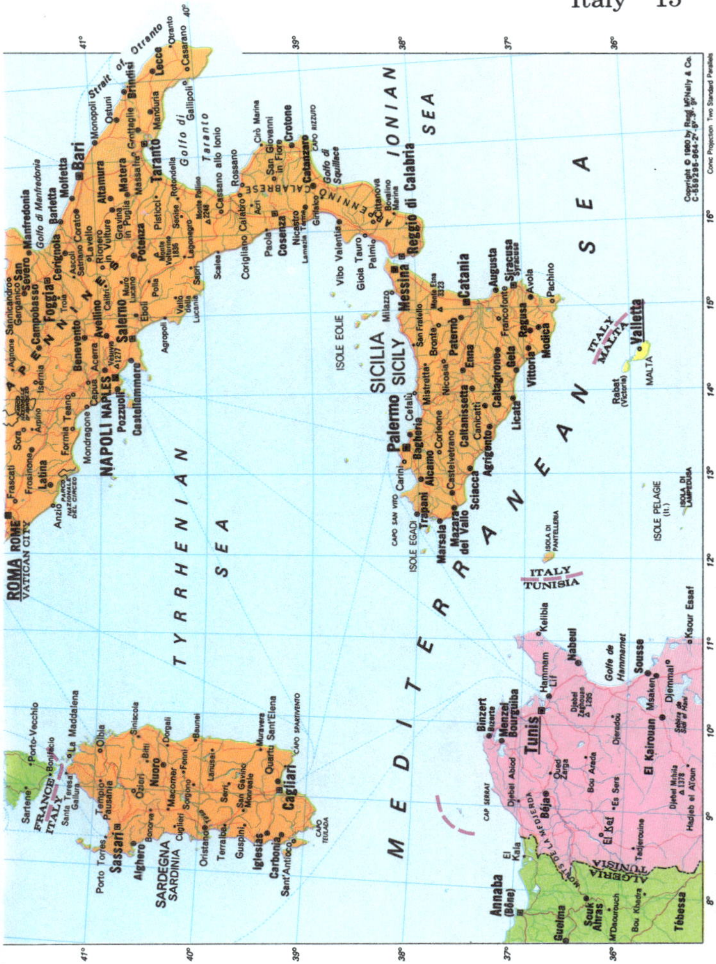
ROMA ROME
VATICAN CITY
TYRRHENIAN SEA
IONIAN SEA
MEDITERRANEAN SEA
SARDEGNA
SARDINIA
SICILIA
SICILY
MALTA
Valletta
ITALY
TUNISIA
ALGERIA
FRANCE
Tunis
Bizerte
Menzel Bourguiba
Hammam Lif
Nabeul
Kelibia
Sousse
Msaken
Djemmal
El Kairouan
Béja
El Kef
Annaba (Bône)
Guelma
Souk Ahras
Tébessa
Golfe de Hammamet
Cagliari
Sassari
Alghero
Porto Torres
Nuoro
Olbia
La Maddalena
Iglesias
Carbonia
Oristano
Tempio Pausania
Palermo
Trapani
Marsala
Mazara del Vallo
Sciacca
Agrigento
Caltanissetta
Enna
Catania
Messina
Siracusa
Syracuse
Ragusa
Modica
Gela
Licata
Augusta
Vittoria
Pachino
Alcamo
Bagheria
Cefalù
ISOLE EOLIE
ISOLE EGADI
ISOLA DI PANTELLERIA
ISOLE PELAGIE (It.)
Reggio di Calabria
Catanzaro
Crotone
Cosenza
Rossano
Golfo di Squillace
Golfo di Taranto
Taranto
Bari
Brindisi
Lecce
Otranto
Strait of Otranto
Gallipoli
Foggia
Manfredonia
Golfo di Manfredonia
Barletta
Molfetta
Altamura
Matera
Potenza
Salerno
Avellino
Benevento
Campobasso
NAPOLI NAPLES
Pozzuoli
Castellammare
Caserta
Capua
Latina
Frosinone
Anzio
Frascati
Cerignola
Copyright © 1980 by Rand McNally & Co.
Conic Projection Two Standard Parallels

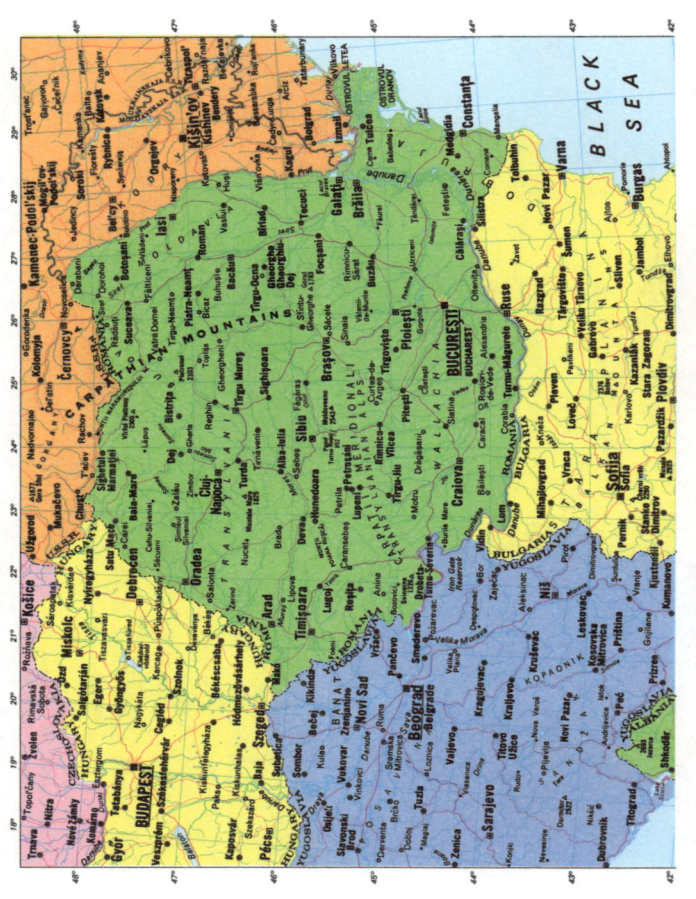

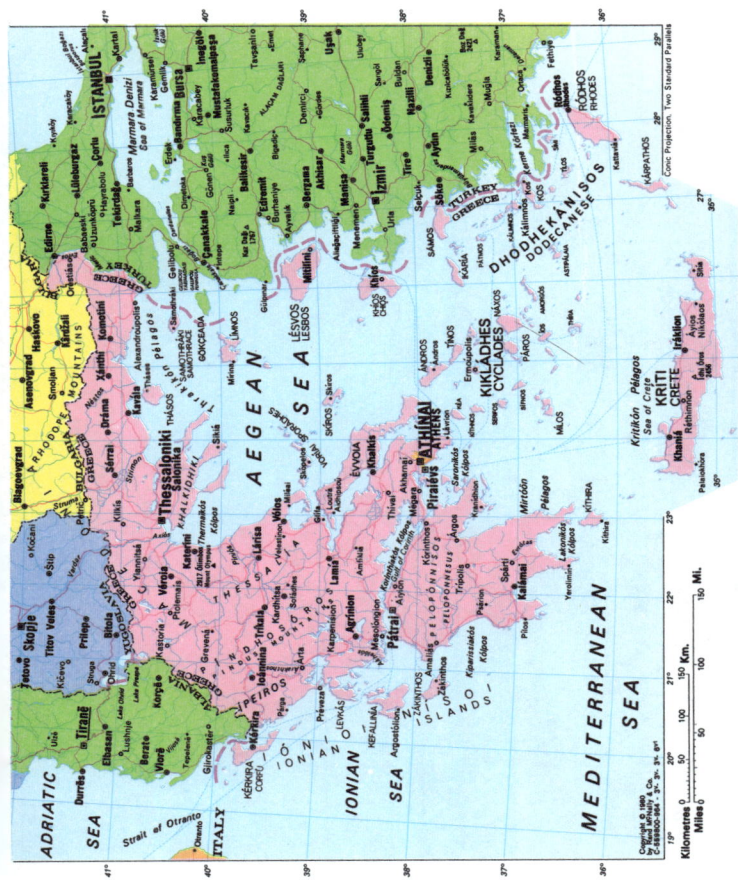

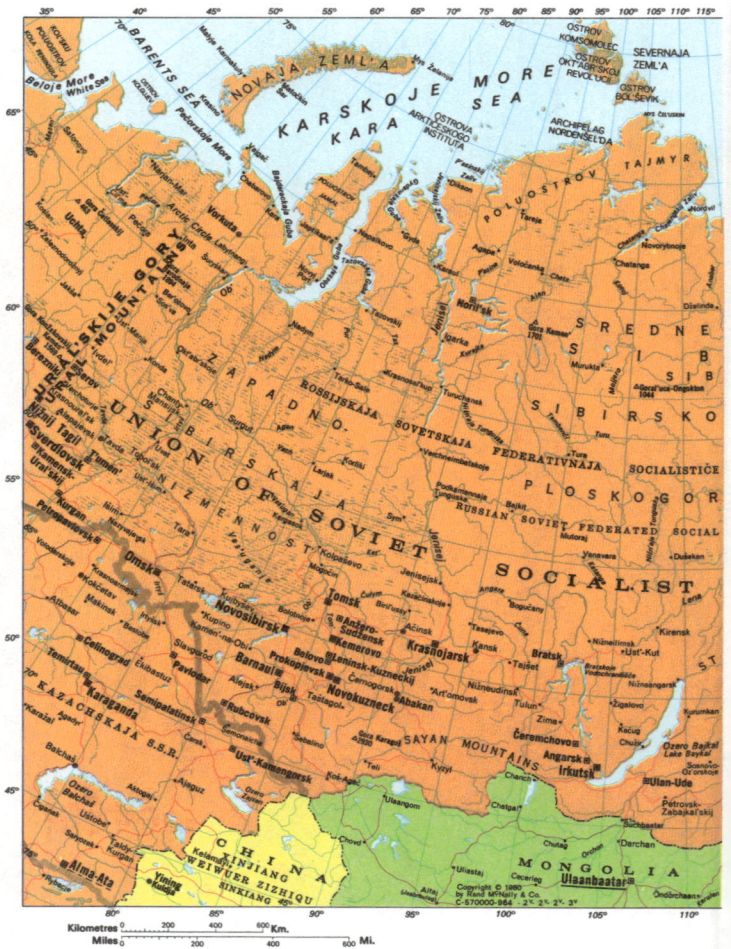

Kilometres 0 200 400 600 Km.

Miles 0 200 400 600 Mi.

MORE LAPTEVYCH

LAPTEV SEA

NOVOSIBIRSKIJE OSTROVA

VOSTOČNO-SIBIRSKOJE MORE
EAST SIBERIAN SEA

OSTROV VRANGELJA

Chukchi Sea

Arctic Circle

EKVATASKIJ CHREBET

Bering Sea

KORJAKSKOJE NAGORJE

CHREBET ČERSKOGO

VERCHOJANSKIJ

CHREBET

Magadan

SEA OF OKHOTSK
OCHOTSKOJE MORE

POLUOSTROV KAMČATKA

Petropavlovsk Kamčatskij

JAKUTSKAJA REPUBLIKA

JAKUTSK

YAKUT REPUBLIC

R E P U B L I C S

OSTROV SACHALIN
SAKHALIN

SICHOTE-ALIN

ŠANTARSKIJE OSTROVA

STANOVOJ CHREBET

ANOVOJE NAGORJE

STANOVOY MOUNTAINS

Komsomol'sk-na-Amure

Chabarovsk

Blagoveščensk

Južno-Sachalinsk

KURIL'SKIJE OSTROVA
KURIL ISLANDS

NEIMENGGU ZIZHIQU
INNER MONGOLIA

HEILONGJIANG

C H I N A

Qiqihaer Tsitsihar

Harbin

Mudanjiang

Ussurijsk

Vladivostok

JILIN

SEA OF JAPAN

Sapporo

HOKKAIDO

JAPAN

HONSHU

PACIFIC OCEAN

Lambert Conformal Conic Projection

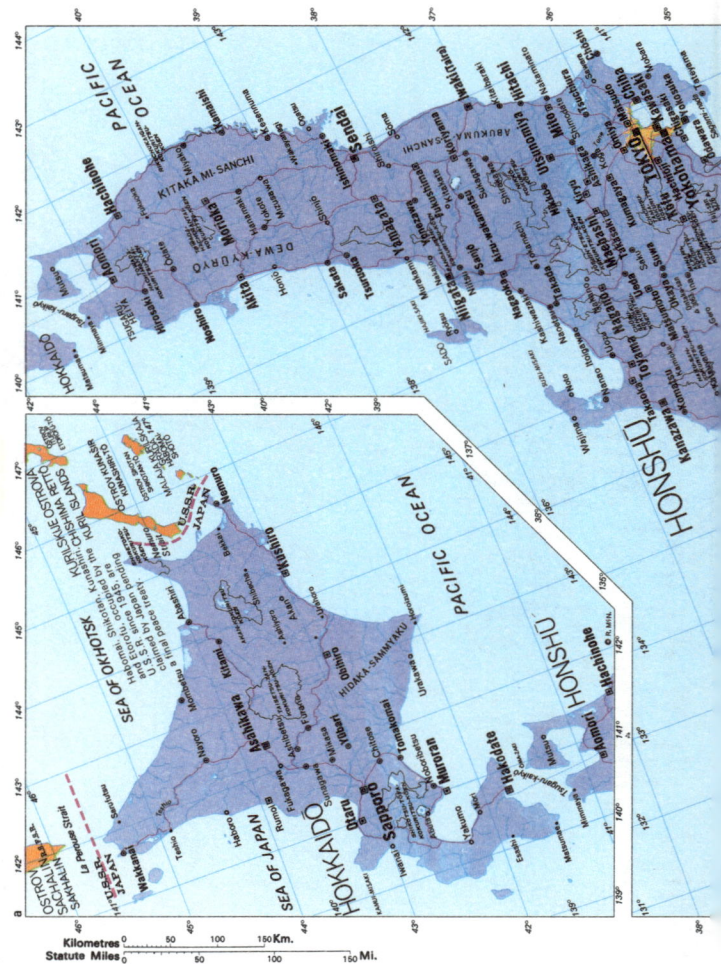

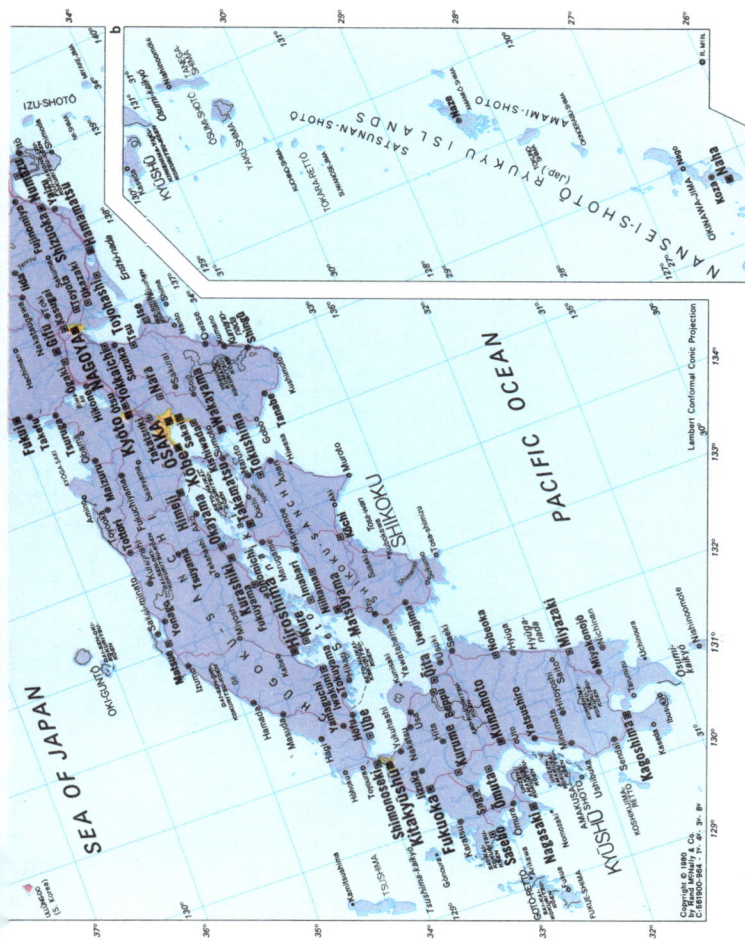

Lambert Conformal Conic Projection

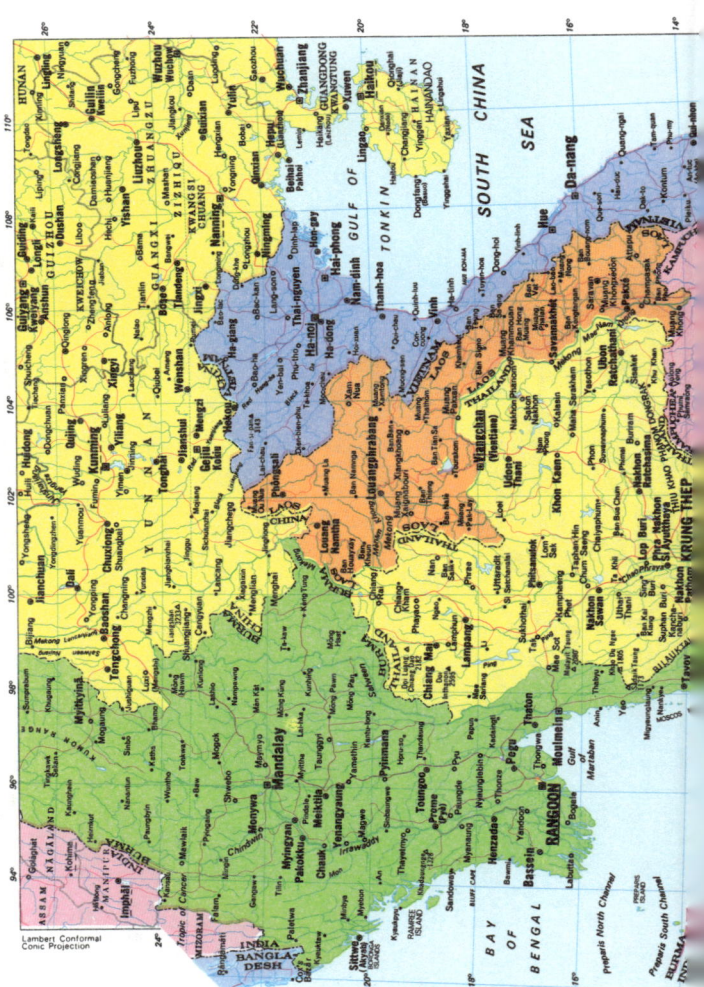

Lambert Conformal
Conic Projection

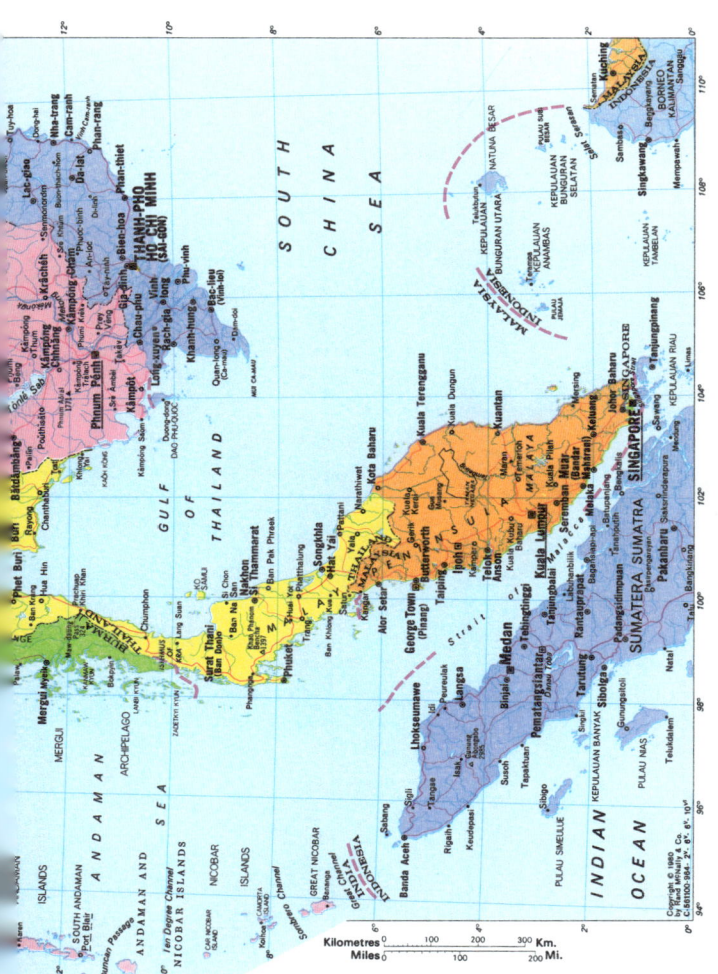

The boundary between India and Pakistan through the disputed state of Jammu and Kashmir follows the "line of control" agreed upon by both countries in 1972.

Copyright © 1980
by Rand McNally & Co.
C-569400-964 - 5° - 5° - 4° - 12°

Kilometres 0   200   400   600 Km.

Miles 0   200   400   600 Mi.

Lambert Conformal
Conic Projection

Miller Oblated Stereographic Projection

INDIAN OCEAN

Equator

SOMALIA
Brava
Afmadú
Gaáhi

IDA
Mbale
Marsabit
Mado
Gashi
KENYA
Eldoret
Kismayu
Lake
Makuru
Victoria
Nairobi
Lamu
Kilimanjaro
5199
TATTA PLATEAU
SERENGETI
PLAIN
Vol
Arusha
Mombasa
MASAI
STEPPE
PEMBA ISLAND
Shinyanga
Tanga
Zanzibar
ZANZIBAR
TANZANIA
Dodoma
Dar es Salaam
Morogoro
Kilwa Kivinje
Iringa
Lindi
Mtwara
Njombe
Masasi
Songea
Mbeya
Lake
Nyasa

SEYCHELLES
Victoria

AMIRANTE ISLANDS
(Sey.)
PLATTE ISLAND (Sey.)

ALPHONSE ISLAND (Sey.)

ALDABRA ISLANDS
(Sey.)
PROVIDENCE ISLAND
(Sey.)

ASTOVE ISLAND
(Sey.)
FARQUHAR GROUP
(Sey.)
AGALEGA ISLANDS
(Mauritius)

MALAWI
Lilongwe
Lichinga
Montepuez
Pemba
NJAZIDJA
Moroni
COMOROS
ILES GLORIEUSES
(Fr.)
CAP D'AMBRE
Antsiranana

Blantyre
Zomba
Mandimba
Malema
Nempula
Mocambique
António Enes

MAYOTTE
(Fr.)
Dzaoudzi
NOSY BE
Andoany
Maromokotro
2876
Iharana

Antalaha

Analalava
Maroantsetra

MOZAMBIQUE
Quelimane
Chinde

Mahajanga
Port-Bergé
Maevatanana
Maroantsetra
Mananara
TROMELIN
(Fr.)

Beira

Besalampy
Marovoay

Tambohorano
Toamasina
Antananarivo

Ankavandra
Antsirabe
Mahanoro

MADAGASCAR
Belo
Malaimbandy
Ambositra
Fianarantsoa

Morondava
Manakara

Mampikony
Maintirano
Belo
Morombe
Beroroha
Pte. Barow
Manakara

Nova Mambone
BASSAS DA INDIA
(Fr.)
Ankazoabo
Vangaindrano

PONTA SÃO SEBASTIÃO
I. EUROPA
(Fr.)
Toliara
Betroka
Midongy
Sud
Bekily

PONTA DA BARRA FALSA

Inhambane
Androka
Faradofay

Xai-Xai
CAP SAINTE-MARIE

MAURITIUS
Port Louis
Saint-Denis
RÉUNION
(Fr.)
MASCARENE
ISLANDS

Tropic of Capricorn

INDIAN OCEAN

Copyright © 1980
by Rand McNally & Co.
C-589200-984 - 5°- 8°- 8°- 15°

Kilometres 0   200   400   600 Km.
Miles 0   200   400   600 Mi.

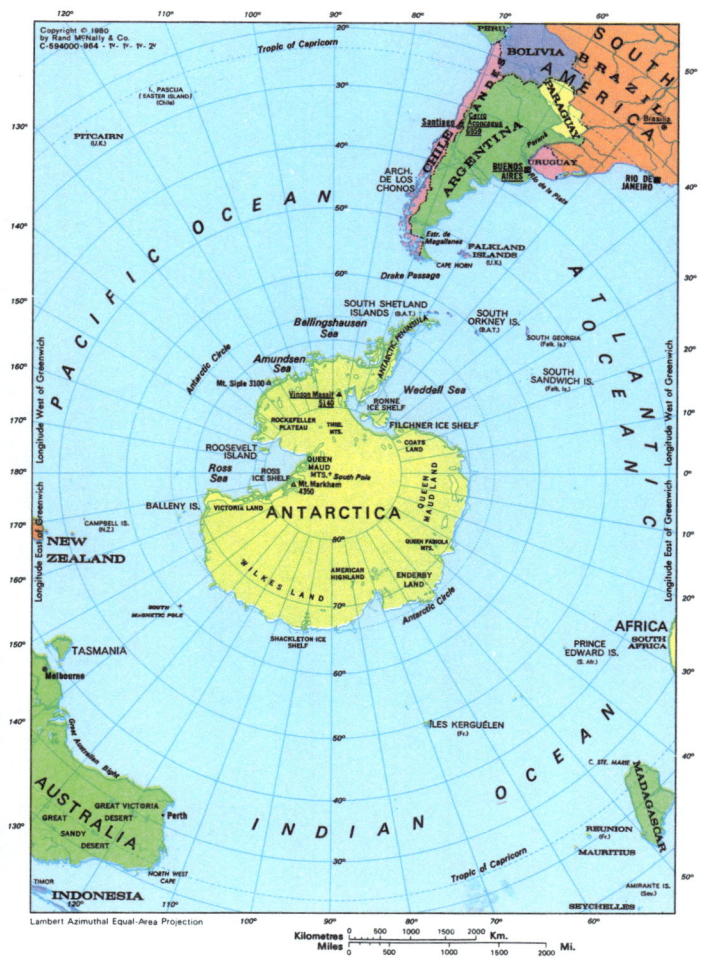

Copyright © 1980
by Rand McNally & Co.
C-594000-964 - 1ᵛ- 1ᵛ- 1ᵛ- 2ᵛ

Lambert Azimuthal Equal-Area Projection

Kilometres 0   200   400   600 Km.
Statute Miles 0   200   400   600 Mi.

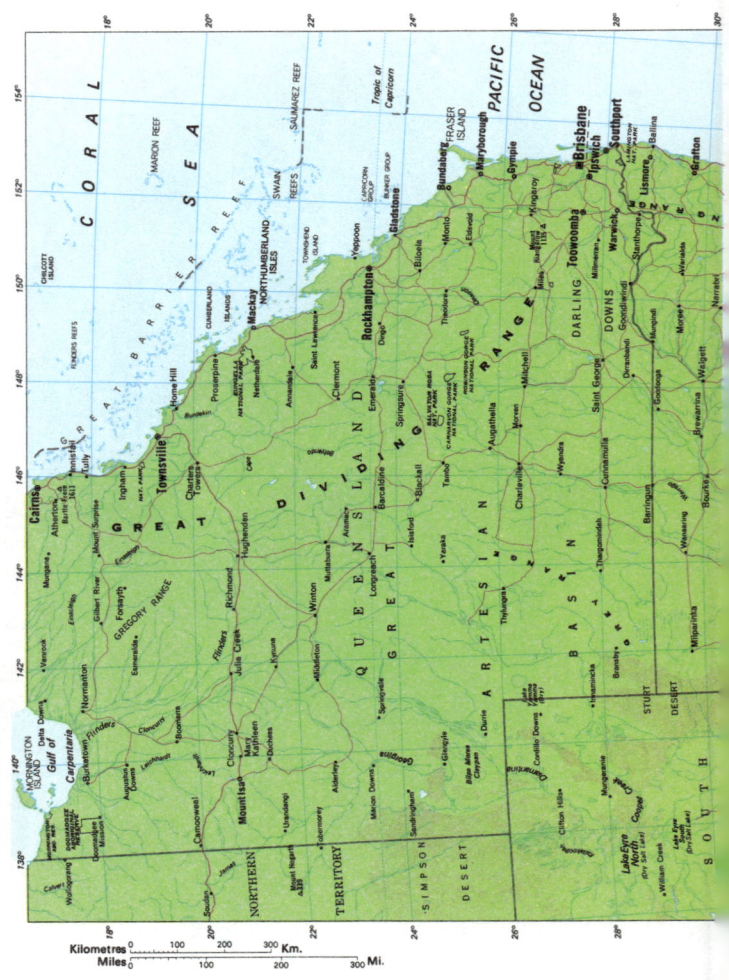

Kilometres 0 100 200 300 Km.
Miles 0 100 200 300 Mi.

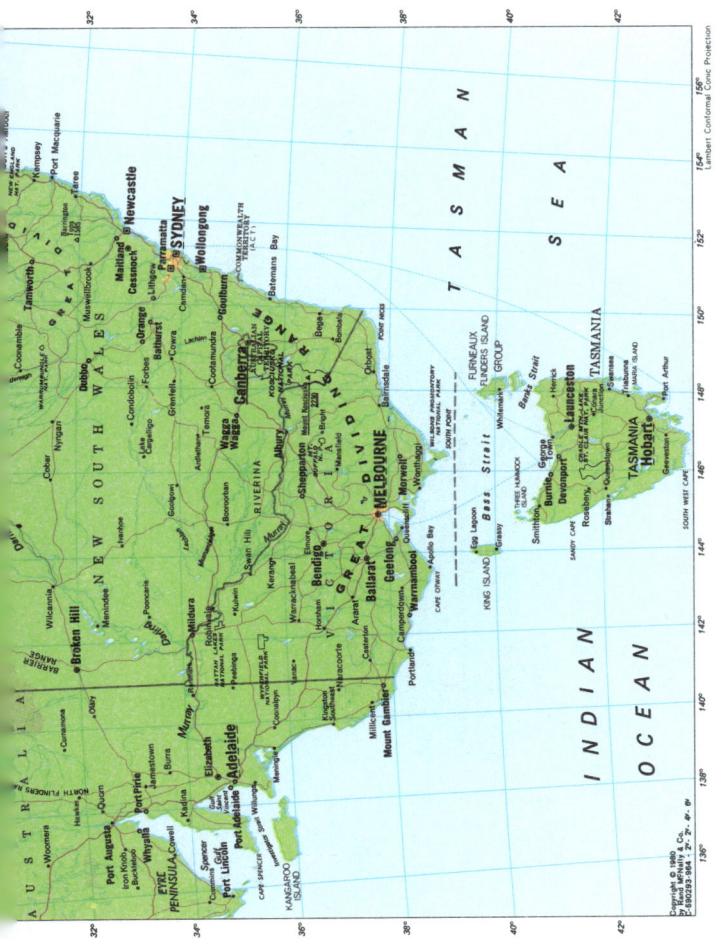

NORTH CAPE

TAUROA POINT

Doubtless Bay

Okaihau

Whangarei

Dargaville

PACIFIC

OCEAN

GREAT
BARRIER
ISLAND

Wellsford

Kaipara
Harbour

Takapuna

Devonport

COROMANDEL
PENINSULA

Auckland

Thames

Waihi

Hamilton

Morrinsville

Tauranga

*Bay of
Plenty*

EAST
CAPE

36°

36°

NORTH

ISLAND

Te Kuiti

Rotorua

Opotiki

Murupara

38°

38°

Taumarunui

Taupo

*Lake
Taupo*

Gisborne

T A S M A N

Ruapehu
△2797

Wairoa

MAHIA
PENINSULA

New Plymouth

Opunake

Raetihi

Napier

*Hawke
Bay*

S E A

Hawera

Taihape

Hastings

Wanganui

Waipukurau

40°

40°

CAPE FAREWELL

Palmerston North

Woodville

D'URVILLE
ISLAND

Levin

Takaka

*Tasman
Bay*

Masterton

Nelson

Cook

Lower Hutt

Karamea
Bight

Blenheim

Wellington

Westport

Tapuaenuku
△2885

Strait

CAPE PALLISER

42°

42°

Reefton

Kaikoura

Greymouth

Hokitika

Waiau

SOUTH

Waipara

Whataroa

Sheffield

Pegasus Bay

ISLAND

Mount Cook
△3764

Christchurch

Haast

Ashburton

BANKS
PENINSULA

CASCADE
POINT

Mount
Aspiring
△3039

Fairlie

*Canterbury
Bight*

44°

44°

Omarama

Timaru

Wanaka

Queenstown

Oamaru

Kingston

Alexandra

Palmerston

PACIFIC

Lake
Te Anau

Mossburn

Beaumont

Dunedin

OCEAN

CAPE
PROVIDENCE

Winton

Gore

Invercargill

Kaitangata

Foveaux

Bluff

46°

**STEWART
ISLAND**

Copyright © 1980
by Rand McNally & Co.
C-591800-964 - 2° - 2° - 4° - 7°

Conic Projection

Kilometres

Miles

Km.

Mi.

*BARBADOS

AND TOBAGO

Morawhanna
Charity
Georgetown
Wismar
New Amsterdam
Roraima
Skeldon
GUYANA
Lethem
Apoteri

ATLANTIC   OCEAN

10°

5°

Paramaribo
ÎLE DU DIABLE
Cayenne
Brokopondo

SURINAME
Juliana Top 1230
FRENCH GUIANA

ACARAI MTS

TUMUC-HUMAC MTS

Cunani
Calçoene   ILHA DE MARACÁ

ILHA CAVIANA

Macapá

Equator

0°

ILHA DE MARAJÓ
Pará
Curuçú
Belém
Cametá
Camimú
Porto de Moz
Santarém
Parintins
Amazonas
Altamira
Amazon
São Luís
Monção
Rosário
Parnaíba
Acaraú
Cametá
Tucuruí
Fortaleza

Icoatiara

Tapajós

Itaituba

Marabá
Bacabal
Barras
Sobral
Betumite
Quixadá
Aracati

ILHA FERNANDO DE NORONHA
(Brazil)

5°

SERRA DO CACHIMBO

Xingu

Tocantinópolis
Gradaús
Barra do Corda
Teresina
Crateús
Senador Pompeu
Mossoró
CABO DE SÃO ROQUE
Currais Novos
Macau
Natal

Floriano
Loreto
Benedito Leite
Picos
Sousa
Juazeiro do Norte
Serra Talhada
Campina Grande
João Pessoa
Olinda
Recife

Araguacema
Carolina
Alto Parnaíba
Paulistana
Remanso
Petrolina
Pesqueira
União dos Palmares
Caruaru

B   R   A   Z   I   L

ILHA DO BANANAL
Gurupi

Paranã
Taguatinga
Passagem
Gilbués
Xique-Xique
São Francisco
Jeremoabo
Maceió

10°

Uiarani
Aracaju

RECIS
PLANALTO DO MATO GROSSO
Porto Nandayu
São Domingos
Posse
Santo Antônio de Jesus
Feira de Santana
Alagoinhas

Aruanã
Carinhanha
Peramim
Jequié
Itabuna
Salvador

Corumbá
Porto Esperança
Cuiabá
Rondonópolis
Alto Araguaia
Jataí
Itumbiara
Goiânia
Brasília
PLANALTO CENTRAL
Montes Claros
Monte Azul
Guanambi
Ilhéus
Canavieiras
Pôrto Seguro

15°

Itabé

SERRA DO RONCADOR
SERRA DO ESPINHAÇO

Corinto
Diamantina
Nanuque
Alcobaça
Vitória da Conquista

Rumbiara
Uberlândia
Sete Lagoas
Governador Valadares
São Mateus
Colatina

UAY
Aquidauana
Puerto Casedo
Campo Grande
Coxim
Uberaba
São José do Rio Prêto
Divinópolis
Belo Horizonte
Vitória

Bela Vista
Presidente Prudente
Araçatuba
Barretos
Ribeirão Prêto
Araraquara
Bauru
Campinas
Volta Redonda
Petrópolis
Campos
RIO DE JANEIRO
Niterói
SÃO PAULO
Juiz de Fora
Santos
Tropic of Capricorn

20°

Oblique Conic Conformal Projection

PACIFIC

OCEAN

Tropic of Cancer

Kilometres
Miles

48

Lambert Conformal Conic Projection

Copyright © 1980
by Rand McNally & Co.
C-520200-964 · 4° · 4° · 6° · 9°

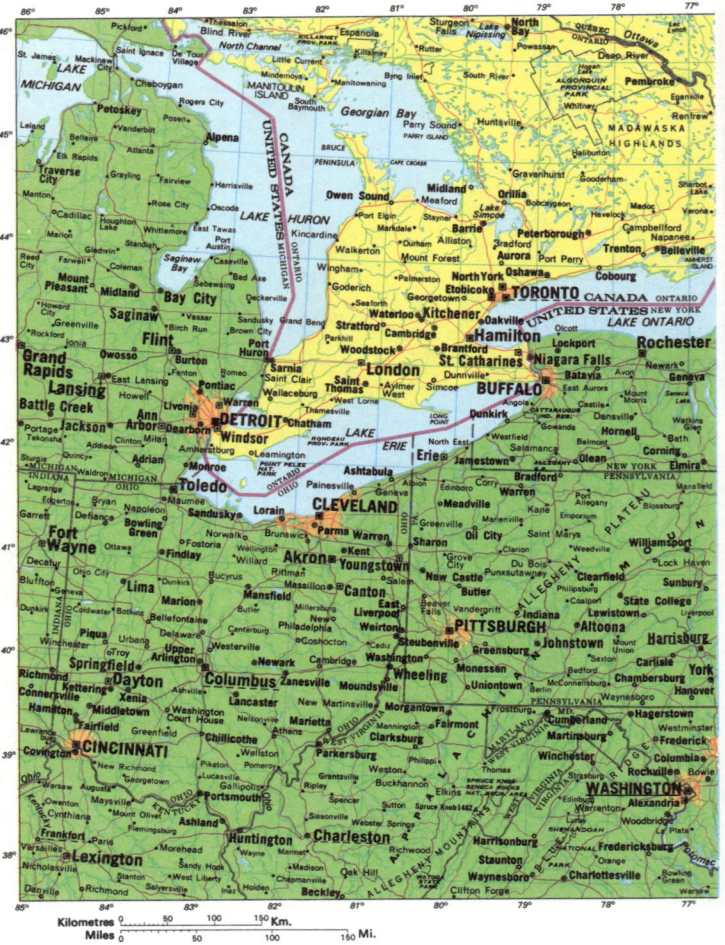

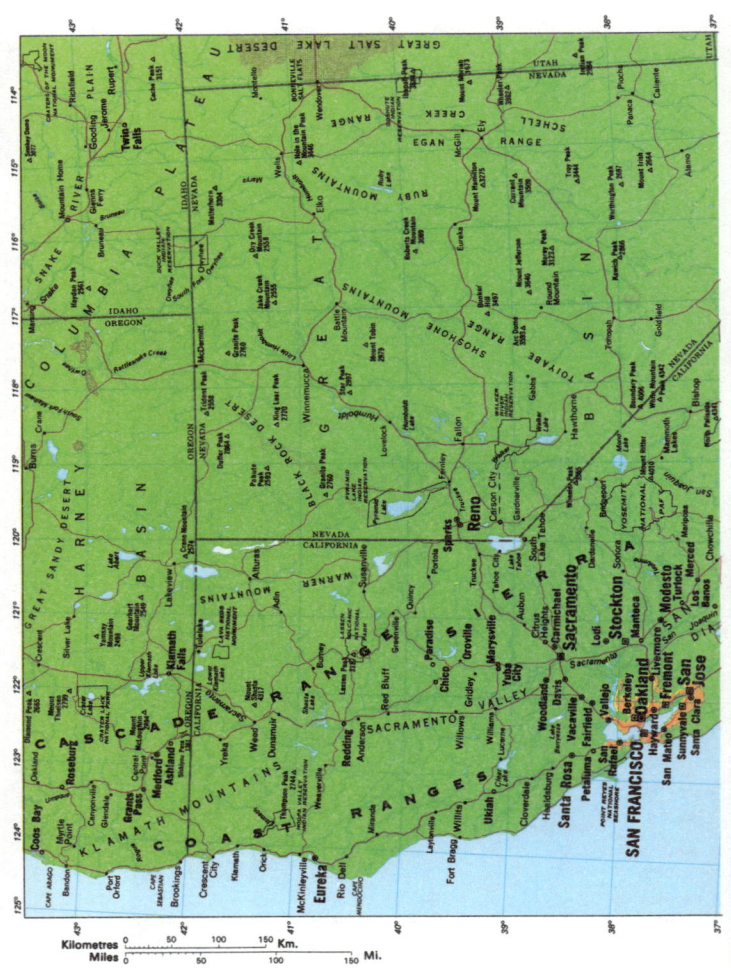

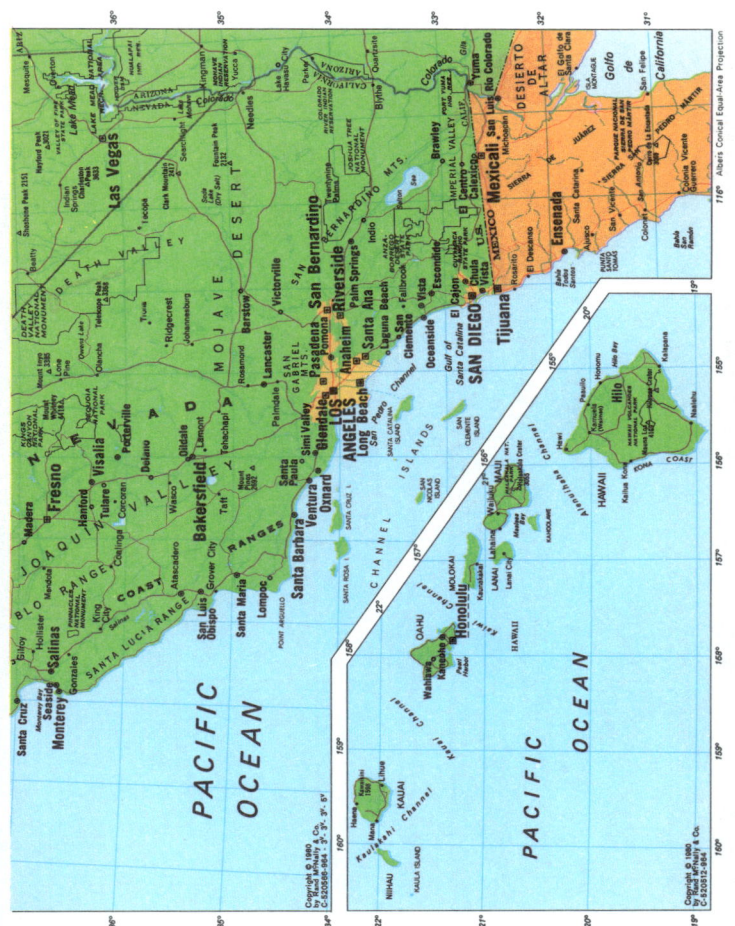

INTRODUCTION TO THE INDEX

Local official names are used on the maps and in the index. Features that extend beyond the boundaries of one country and have no single official name are usually named in English. Many conventional English names and former names are cross-referenced to the official names.

The names of physical features may appear inverted, since they are always alphabetized under the proper, not the generic, part of the name, thus: "Gibraltar, Strait of ʊ". Otherwise every entry, whether consisting of one word or more, is alphabetized as a single continuous entity. "La Habana," for example, appears after "Lagos" and before "Lahore." Names beginning with articles (Al-Qāhirah, Ad-Dawhah) are not inverted. Names beginning "Mc" are alphabetized as though spelled "Mac" and names beginning "St.", as though spelled "Saint." Entries that are completely identical (including symbols, discussed below) are distinguished by abbreviations of their official country names. The country abbreviations used for places in the United States, Canada and United Kingdom indicate the state, province or political division in which the feature is located. (See List of Abbreviations below.)

City names are not followed by symbols. The names of all other features are followed by symbols that graphically represent kinds of features, for example, ʌ for mountain (Everest, Mount ʌ). A complete list of symbols follows the List of Abbreviations. All cross-references are indicated by the symbol →.

Page references to two-page maps always refer to the left-hand page. If a page contains several maps or insets, a lowercase letter identifies the specific map or inset.

ABBREVIATIONS

Al., U.S.	Alabama	**Guy.**	Guyana
B.C., Can.	British Columbia	**H.K.**	Hong Kong
		S.C., U.S.	South Carolina
Cay. Is.	Cayman Islands	**Sey.**	Seychelles
Eng., U.K.	England	**W.V., U.S.**	West Virginia

SYMBOLS

ʌ	**Mountain**	±	**Other Topographic Features**	ᴛ	**Other Hydrographic Features**	□³	State, Canton, Republic
ʌ¹	Volcano					□⁴	Province, Region, Oblast
⋌	**Mountains**	±¹	Continent	ᴛ¹	Ocean	□⁸	Miscellaneous
)(	**Pass**	≃	**River**	ᴛ²	Sea	□⁹	Historical
V	**Valley, Canyon**	ʊ	**Strait**	□	**Political Unit**	←	**Miscellaneous**
>	**Cape**	c	**Bay, Gulf**	□¹	Independent Nation	←¹	Region
>¹	Peninsula	ᴓ	**Lake, Lakes**	□²	Dependency	←²	Desert
I	**Island**						
II	**Islands**						

Name	Page No.	Lat.	Long.
Brasilia	42	15.47 S	47.55 W
Brazil □ ¹	42	10.00 S	55.00 W
Brazzaville	32	4.16 S	5.17 E
Bridgetown	44	13.06 N	59.37 W
British Columbia □ ⁴	48	54.00 N	125.00 W
Brunei □ ¹	24	4.30 N	114.40 E
Brussels			
→ Bruxelles	8	50.50 N	4.20 E
Bruxelles (Brussel)	8	50.50 N	4.20 E
Bucureşti (Bucharest)	16	44.26 N	26.06 E
Budapest	8	47.30 N	19.05 E
Buenos Aires	41	34.36 S	58.27 W
Bujumbura	32	3.23 S	29.22 E
Bulgaria □ ¹	4	43.00 N	25.00 E
Burkina Faso □ ¹	30	13.00 N	2.00 W
Burma □ ¹	24	22.00 N	98.00 E
Burundi □ ¹	32	3.15 S	30.00 E

C

Cairo			
→ Al-Qāhirah	30	30.03 N	31.15 E
Calcutta	28	22.34 N	88.20 E
Calgary	48	51.03 N	114.05 W
California □ ³	50	37.30 N	119.30 W
California, Golfo de c	46	28.00 N	112.00 W
Cambodia			
→ Kampuchea □ ¹	24	13.00 N	105.00 E
Cameroon □ ¹	30	6.00 N	12.00 E
Canada □ ¹	48	60.00 N	95.00 W
Canarias, Islas (Canary Islands) II	30	28.00 N	15.30 W
Canaveral, Cape ▸	50	28.27 N	80.32 W
Canberra	36	35.17 S	149.08 E
Canton			
→ Guangzhou	20	23.06 N	113.16 E
Cape Town (Kaapstad)	32	33.55 S	18.22 E
Caracas	42	10.30 N	66.56 W
Cardiff	6	51.29 N	3.13 W
Caribbean Sea ⊤ ²	44	15.00 N	73.00 W
Carpathian Mountains ⋏	4	48.00 N	24.00 E
Carson City	54	39.10 N	119.46 W
Casablanca (Dar-el-Beida)	30	33.39 N	7.35 W
Cascade Range ⋏	50	49.00 N	120.00 W
Caspian Sea ⊤ ²	4	42.00 N	50.30 E
Castries	44	14.01 N	61.00 W
Caucasus			
→ Bol'šoj Kavkaz ⋏	4	42.30 N	45.00 E
Cayenne	42	4.56 N	52.20 W
Cayman Islands □ ²	24	19.30 N	80.40 W
Cebu	24	10.18 N	123.54 E
Celebes			
→ Sulawesi I	24	2.00 S	121.00 E
Central African Republic □ ¹	30	7.00 N	21.00 E
Chad □ ¹	30	15.00 N	19.00 E
Changjiang (Yangtze) ≃	20	31.48 N	121.10 E
Char'kov	4	50.00 N	36.15 E
Charleston, S.C., U.S.	50	32.46 N	79.55 W
Charleston, W.V., U.S.	52	38.20 N	81.37 W
Charlotte Amalie	44	18.21 N	64.56 W
Charlottetown	48	46.14 N	63.08 W
Cheyenne	50	41.08 N	104.49 W
Chicago	50	41.51 N	87.39 W
Chile □ ¹	41	30.00 S	71.00 W
China □ ¹	20	35.00 N	105.00 E
Christchurch	40	43.32 S	172.38 E
Cincinnati	52	39.09 N	84.27 W

Name	Page No.	Lat.	Long.
Ciudad de México (Mexico City)	46	19.24 N	99.09 W
Ciudad Juárez	46	31.44 N	106.29 W
Cleveland	52	41.29 N	81.41 W
Coast Ranges ⋏	50	41.00 N	123.30 W
Cologne			
→ Köln	8	50.56 N	6.59 E
Colombia □ ¹	42	4.00 N	72.00 W
Colombo	28	6.56 N	79.51 E
Colorado □ ³	50	39.30 N	105.30 W
Colorado ≃	50	31.54 N	114.57 W
Columbia	50	34.00 N	81.02 W
Columbia ≃	48	46.15 N	124.05 W
Columbus	52	39.57 N	82.59 W
Comoros □ ¹	32	12.10 S	44.10 E
Conakry	30	9.31 N	13.43 W
Concord	52	43.12 N	71.32 W
Congo □ ¹	32	1.00 S	15.00 E
Congo (Zaïre) ≃	32	6.04 S	12.24 E
Connecticut □ ³	52	41.45 N	72.45 W
Cook Islands □ ²	2	20.00 S	158.00 W
Copenhagen			
→ København	7	55.40 N	12.35 E
Coral Sea ⊤ ²	2	20.00 S	158.00 E
Cork	6	51.54 N	8.28 W
Corse (Corsica) I	14	42.00 N	9.00 E
Costa Rica □ ¹	44	10.00 N	84.00 W
Crete			
→ Kríti I	16	35.29 N	24.42 E
Cuba □ ¹	44	21.30 N	80.00 W
Cyprus □ ¹	29	35.00 N	33.00 E
Czechoslovakia □ ¹	4	49.30 N	17.00 E

D

Dakar	30	14.40 N	17.26 W
Dallas	50	32.46 N	96.47 W
Damascus			
→ Dimashq	29	33.30 N	36.18 E
Danube (Donau) (Dunaj) (Duna) ≃	8	45.20 N	29.40 E
Dar es Salaam	32	6.48 S	39.17 E
Dead Sea ⊜	29	31.30 N	35.30 E
Death Valley V	54	36.30 N	117.00 W
Delaware □ ³	50	39.10 N	75.30 W
Denmark □ ¹	4	56.00 N	10.00 E
Denver	50	39.44 N	104.59 W
Des Moines	50	41.36 N	93.36 W
Detroit	52	42.20 N	83.03 W
Dhaka	28	23.43 N	90.25 E
Dimashq (Damascus)	29	33.30 N	36.18 E
Djibouti □ ¹	34	11.30 N	43.00 E
Doha			
→ Ad-Dawhah	34	25.17 N	51.32 E
Dominica □ ¹	44	15.30 N	61.20 W
Dominican Republic □ ¹	44	19.00 N	70.40 W
Douglas	6	54.09 N	4.28 W
Dover, Strait of (Pas de Calais) ม	10	51.00 N	1.30 E
Dresden	8	51.03 N	13.44 E
Dublin (Baile Átha Cliath)	6	53.20 N	6.15 W
Durban	32	29.55 S	30.56 E

E

Ecuador □ ¹	42	2.00 S	77.30 W
Edinburgh	6	55.57 N	3.13 W
Edmonton	48	53.33 N	113.28 W
Egypt □ ¹	30	27.00 N	30.00 E

Name	Page No.	Lat.	Long.
El Aaiún	30	27.09N	13.12W
El Salvador □¹	44	13.50N	88.55W
England □⁸	6	52.30N	1.30W
English Channel (La Manche) ⅃⅃	10	50.20N	1.00W
Equatorial Guinea □¹	30	2.00N	9.00 E
Erie, Lake ⊜	50	42.15N	81.00W
Ethiopia □¹	34	9.00N	39.00 E
Etna, Monte ∧¹	14	37.46N	15.00 E
Euphrates (Al-Furāt) ≃	34	31.00N	47.25 E
Europe ⅃¹	2	50.00N	20.00 E
Everest, Mount (Zhumulangmafeng) ∧	28	27.59N	86.56 E

F

Name	Page No.	Lat.	Long.
Faeroe Islands □²	4	62.00N	7.00W
Falkland Islands □²	41	51.45S	59.00W
Fiji □¹	2	18.00S	175.00W
Finland □¹	4	64.00N	26.00 E
Firenze (Florence)	14	43.46N	11.15 E
Florence → Firenze	14	43.46N	11.15 E
Florida □³	50	28.00N	82.00W
Fort-de-France	44	14.36N	61.05W
Fort Worth	50	32.43N	97.19W
France □¹	4	46.00N	2.00 E
Frankfort	50	38.12N	84.52W
Frankfurt am Main	8	50.07N	8.40 E
Fredericton	48	45.58N	66.39W
Freetown	30	8.30N	13.15W
French Guiana □²	42	4.00N	53.00W
French Polynesia □²	2	15.00S	140.00W

G

Name	Page No.	Lat.	Long.
Gabon □¹	32	1.00S	11.45 E
Gaborone	32	24.45S	25.55 E
Gambia □¹	30	13.30N	15.30W
Ganges (Ganga) (Padma) ≃	28	23.22N	90.32 E
Gdańsk (Danzig)	8	54.23N	18.40 E
Genova (Genoa)	14	44.25N	8.57 E
Georgetown, Cay. Is.	44	19.18N	81.23W
Georgetown, Guy.	42	6.48N	58.10W
Georgia □³	50	32.50N	83.15W
German Democratic Republic (East Germany) □¹	4	52.00N	12.30 E
Germany, Federal Republic of (West Germany) □¹	4	51.00N	9.00 E
Ghana □¹	30	8.00N	2.00W
Gibraltar □²	4	36.11N	5.22W
Gibraltar, Strait of (Estrecho de Gibraltar) ⅃⅃	12	35.57N	5.36W
Glasgow	6	55.53N	4.15W
Gobi ◆²	20	43.00N	105.00 E
Godthåb	2	64.11N	51.44W
Gor'kij	4	56.20N	44.00 E
Grande, Rio (Bravo del Norte) ≃	50	25.55N	97.09W
Grand Turk	44	21.28N	71.08W
Greater Antilles ⅃⅃	44	20.00N	74.00W
Great Salt Lake ⊜	50	41.10N	112.30W
Greece □¹	4	39.00N	22.00 E
Greenland □²	2	70.00N	40.00W
Grenada □¹	44	12.07N	61.40W
Guadeloupe □²	44	16.15N	61.35W

Name	Page No.	Lat.	Long.
Guam □²	24	13.28N	144.47 E
Guangzhou (Canton)	20	23.06N	113.16 E
Guatemala	44	14.38N	90.31W
Guatemala □¹	44	15.30N	90.15W
Guayaquil	42	2.10S	79.50W
Guinea □¹	30	11.00N	10.00W
Guinea-Bissau □¹	30	12.00N	15.00W
Guyana □¹	42	5.00N	59.00W

H

Name	Page No.	Lat.	Long.
Haiti □¹	44	19.00N	72.25W
Halifax	48	44.39N	63.36W
Hamburg	8	53.33N	9.59 E
Hamilton	50	32.17N	64.46W
Ha-noi	26	21.02N	105.51 E
Harare	32	17.50S	31.03 E
Harbin	20	45.45N	126.41 E
Harrisburg	52	40.16N	76.53W
Hartford	52	41.46N	72.41W
Havana → La Habana	44	23.08N	82.22W
Hawaii □³	55a	20.00N	157.45W
Hebrides ⅃⅃	4	57.00N	6.30W
Helena	50	46.35N	112.02W
Helsinki (Helsingfors)	7	60.10N	24.58 E
Himalayas ◆	28	30.00N	84.00 E
Hiroshima	22	34.24N	132.27 E
Hokkaidō I	22a	44.00N	143.00 E
Honduras □¹	44	15.00N	86.30W
Hong Kong □²	20	22.15N	114.10 E
Honiara	36	9.26S	159.57 E
Honolulu	55a	21.18N	157.51W
Honshū I	22	36.00N	138.00 E
Hornos, Cabo de (Cape Horn) ►	41	55.59S	67.16W
Houston	50	29.45N	95.21W
Huanghe ≃	20	37.32N	118.19 E
Hudson ≃	52	40.42N	74.02W
Hudson Bay ⊂	48	60.00N	86.00W
Hungary □¹	4	47.00N	20.00 E
Huron, Lake ⊜	50	44.30N	82.15W
Hyderābād	28	17.23N	78.29 E

I

Name	Page No.	Lat.	Long.
Ibadan	30	7.17N	3.30 E
Iceland □¹	4	65.00N	18.00W
Idaho □³	50	45.00N	115.00W
Illinois □³	50	40.00N	89.00W
India □¹	28	20.00N	77.00 E
Indiana □³	50	40.00N	86.15W
Indianapolis	50	39.46N	86.09W
Indian Ocean ⅃⁻¹	2	10.00S	70.00 E
Indonesia □¹	24	5.00S	120.00 E
Indus ≃	28	24.20N	67.47 E
Iowa □³	50	42.15N	93.15W
Iran □¹	2	32.00N	53.00 E
Iraq □¹	34	33.00N	44.00 E
Ireland □¹	4	53.00N	8.00W
Islāmābād	28	33.42N	73.10 E
Israel □¹	29	31.30N	35.00 E
İstanbul	16	41.01N	28.58 E
Italy □¹	4	42.50N	12.50 E
Ivory Coast □¹	30	8.00N	5.00W

J

Name	Page No.	Lat.	Long.
Jackson	50	32.17N	90.11W
Jakarta	24	6.10S	106.48 E
Jamaica □¹	44	18.15N	77.30W

Name	Page No.	Lat.	Long.
Japan □ ¹	20	36.00 N	138.00 E
Jawa (Java) I	24	7.30 S	110.00 E
Jefferson City	50	38.34 N	92.10 W
Jerusalem → Yerushalayim	29	31.46 N	35.14 E
Johannesburg	32	26.15 S	28.00 E
Jordan □ ¹	29	31.00 N	36.00 E
Juneau	56	58.20 N	134.27 W
K			
K2 ʌ	28	35.53 N	76.30 E
Kābul	28	34.30 N	69.11 E
Kampala	32	0.19 N	32.25 E
Kampuchea □ ¹	24	13.00 N	105.00 E
Kansas □ ³	50	38.45 N	98.15 W
Karāchi	28	24.52 N	67.03 E
Kathmandu	28	27.43 N	85.19 E
Kentucky □ ³	50	37.30 N	85.15 W
Kenya □ ¹	32	1.00 N	38.00 E
Kharkov → Char'kov	4	50.00 N	36.15 E
Khartoum → Al-Khartūm	30	15.36 N	32.32 E
Khyber Pass)(	28	34.05 N	71.10 E
Kigali	32	1.57 S	30.04 E
Kijev	4	50.26 N	30.31 E
Kingston	44	18.00 N	76.48 W
Kingstown	44	13.09 N	61.14 W
Kinshasa (Léopoldville)	32	4.18 S	15.18 E
Kiribati □ ¹	2	4.00 S	175.00 E
København (Copenhagen)	7	55.40 N	12.35 E
Köln (Cologne)	8	50.56 N	6.59 E
Korea, North □ ¹	20	40.00 N	127.00 E
Korea, South □ ¹	20	36.30 N	128.00 E
Kríti I	16	35.29 N	24.42 E
Krung Thep (Bangkok)	26	13.45 N	100.31 E
Kuala Lumpur	26	3.10 N	101.42 E
Kujbyšev	4	53.12 N	50.09 E
Kuwait □ ¹	34	29.30 N	47.45 E
Kyūshū I	22	33.00 N	131.00 E
L			
Lagos	30	6.27 N	3.24 E
La Habana (Havana)	44	23.08 N	82.22 W
Lahore	28	31.35 N	74.18 E
Lansing	52	42.43 N	84.33 W
Laos □ ¹	24	18.00 N	105.00 E
La Paz	42	16.30 S	68.09 W
Las Vegas	54	36.10 N	115.08 W
Lebanon □ ¹	29	33.50 N	35.50 E
Leipzig	8	51.19 N	12.20 E
Lena ≃	18	72.25 N	126.40 E
Leningrad	4	59.55 N	30.15 E
Lesotho □ ¹	32	29.30 S	28.30 E
Lhasa	20	29.40 N	91.09 E
Liberia □ ¹	30	6.00 N	10.00 W
Libreville	32	0.23 N	9.27 E
Libya □ ¹	30	27.00 N	17.00 E
Liechtenstein □ ¹	4	47.09 N	9.35 E
Lilongwe	32	13.59 S	33.44 E
Lima	42	12.03 S	77.03 W
Lincoln	50	40.48 N	96.40 W
Lisboa (Lisbon)	12	38.43 N	9.08 W
Little Rock	50	34.44 N	92.17 W
Liverpool	6	53.25 N	2.55 W
Logan, Mount ʌ	48	60.34 N	140.24 W
Lomé	30	6.08 N	1.13 E

Name	Page No.	Lat.	Long.
London	6	51.30 N	0.10 W
Londonderry	6	55.00 N	7.19 W
Los Angeles	54	34.03 N	118.14 W
Louisiana □ ³	50	31.15 N	92.15 W
Louisville	50	38.15 N	85.45 W
Luanda	32	8.48 S	13.14 E
Lusaka	32	15.25 S	28.17 E
Luxembourg □ ¹	4	49.45 N	6.05 E
Luzon I	24	16.00 N	121.00 E
Lyon	10	45.45 N	4.51 E
M			
Macau □ ²	20	22.10 N	113.33 E
McKinley, Mount ʌ	56	63.30 N	151.00 W
Madagascar □ ¹	32	19.00 S	46.00 E
Madison	50	43.04 N	89.24 W
Madras	28	13.04 N	80.16 E
Madrid	12	40.24 N	3.41 W
Magallanes, Estrecho de (Strait of Magellan) ⋃	41	54.00 S	71.00 W
Maine □ ³	50	45.15 N	69.15 W
Makkah (Mecca)	34	21.27 N	39.49 E
Malabo	30	3.45 N	8.47 E
Malawi □ ¹	32	13.30 S	34.00 E
Malaysia □ ¹	24	2.30 N	112.30 E
Mali □ ¹	30	17.00 N	4.00 W
Malta □ ¹	4	35.50 N	14.35 E
Managua	44	12.09 N	86.17 W
Manchester	6	53.30 N	2.15 W
Mandalay	26	22.00 N	96.05 E
Manila	24	14.35 N	121.00 E
Manitoba □ ⁴	48	54.00 N	97.00 W
Maputo (Lourenço Marques)	32	25.58 S	32.35 E
Marseille	10	43.18 N	5.24 E
Martinique □ ²	44	14.40 N	61.00 W
Maryland □ ³	50	39.00 N	76.45 W
Masqat (Muscat)	34	23.37 N	58.35 E
Massachusetts □ ³	50	42.15 N	71.50 W
Matterhorn ʌ	10	45.59 N	7.43 E
Mauritania □ ¹	30	20.00 N	12.00 W
Mauritius □ ¹	32	20.17 S	57.33 E
Mayotte □ ²	32	12.50 S	45.10 E
Mbabane	32	26.18 S	31.06 E
Mecca → Makkah	34	21.27 N	39.49 E
Mediterranean Sea ᵀ ²	2	35.00 N	20.00 E
Mekong ≃	26	10.33 N	105.24 E
Melbourne	36	37.49 S	144.58 E
Memphis	50	35.08 N	90.02 W
Mexico □ ¹	46	23.00 N	102.00 W
Mexico, Gulf of c	46	24.00 N	93.00 W
Mexico City → Ciudad de México	46	19.24 N	99.09 W
Miami	50	25.46 N	80.11 W
Michigan □ ³	50	44.00 N	85.00 W
Michigan, Lake @	50	44.00 N	87.00 W
Milano (Milan)	14	45.28 N	9.12 E
Milwaukee	50	43.02 N	87.54 W
Mindanao I	24	8.00 N	125.00 E
Minneapolis	50	44.58 N	93.15 W
Minnesota □ ³	50	46.00 N	94.15 W
Mississippi □ ³	50	32.50 N	89.30 W
Mississippi ≃	50	29.00 N	89.15 W
Missouri □ ³	50	38.30 N	93.30 W
Missouri ≃	50	38.50 N	90.08 W
Monaco □ ¹	4	43.45 N	7.25 E

Name	Page No.	Lat.	Long.
Mongolia □¹	20	46.00N	105.00 E
Monrovia	30	6.18N	10.47W
Montana □³	50	47.00N	110.00W
Monterrey	46	25.40N	100.19W
Montevideo	41	34.53S	56.11W
Montgomery	50	32.23N	86.18W
Montpelier	52	44.15N	72.34W
Montréal	52	45.31N	73.34W
Montserrat □²	44	16.45N	62.12W
Morocco □¹	30	32.00N	5.00W
Moroni	32	11.41S	43.16 E
Moskva (Moscow)	4	55.45N	37.35 E
Mozambique □¹	32	18.15S	35.00 E
München (Munich)	8	48.08N	11.34 E
Muqdisho	34	2.01N	45.20 E
Murmansk	4	68.58N	33.05 E
Muscat → Masqat	34	23.37N	58.35 E

N

Name	Page No.	Lat.	Long.
Nagoya	22	35.10N	136.55 E
Nairobi	32	1.17S	36.49 E
Namibia □²	32	22.00S	17.00 E
Nanjing (Nanking)	20	32.03N	118.47 E
Napoli (Naples)	14	40.51N	14.17 E
Nashville	50	36.09N	86.47W
Nassau	44	25.05N	77.21W
N'Djamena (Fort-Lamy)	30	12.07N	15.03 E
Nebraska □³	50	41.30N	100.00W
Nepal □¹	28	28.00N	84.00 E
Netherlands □¹	4	52.15N	5.30 E
Netherlands Antilles □²	44	12.15N	69.00W
Neutral Zone □²	34	29.10N	45.30 E
Nevada □³	50	39.00N	117.00W
Newark	52	40.44N	74.10W
New Brunswick □⁴	48	46.30N	66.15W
New Delhi	28	28.36N	77.15 E
Newfoundland □⁴	48	52.00N	56.00W
New Guinea I	24	5.00S	140.00 E
New Hampshire □³	50	43.35N	71.40W
New Jersey □³	50	40.15N	74.30W
New Mexico □³	50	34.30N	106.00W
New Orleans	50	29.57N	90.04W
New York	52	40.43N	74.01W
New York □³	50	43.00N	75.00W
New Zealand □¹	40	41.00S	174.00 E
Niamey	30	13.31N	2.07 E
Nicaragua □¹	44	13.00N	85.00W
Nice	10	43.42N	7.15 E
Nicosia	29	35.10N	33.22 E
Niger □¹	30	16.00N	8.00 E
Niger ≃	30	5.33N	6.33 E
Nigeria □¹	30	10.00N	8.00 E
Nile (Nahr an-Nīl) ≃	30	30.10N	31.06 E
Norfolk	50	36.50N	76.17W
Normandie □⁹	10	49.00N	0.05W
North America ±¹	2	45.00N	100.00W
North Carolina □³	50	35.30N	80.00W
North Dakota □³	50	47.30N	100.15W
Northern Ireland □⁸	6	54.40N	6.45W
North Sea ▼²	4	55.20N	3.00 E
Northwest Territories □⁴	48	70.00N	100.00W
Norway □¹	4	62.00N	10.00 E
Nouakchott	30	18.06N	15.57W
Novaja Zeml'a II	18	74.00N	57.00 E
Nova Scotia □⁴	48	45.00N	63.00W
Novosibirsk	18	55.02N	82.55 E

Name	Page No.	Lat.	Long.
Nürnberg	8	49.27N	11.04 E

O

Name	Page No.	Lat.	Long.
Oahu I	55a	21.30N	158.00W
Oder (Odra) ≃	8	53.32N	14.38 E
Ohio □³	50	40.15N	82.45W
Ohio ≃	50	36.59N	89.08W
Oklahoma □³	50	35.30N	98.00W
Oklahoma City	50	35.28N	97.30W
Olympia	50	47.02N	122.53W
Omaha	50	41.15N	95.56W
Oman □¹	34	22.00N	58.00 E
Ontario □⁴	48	51.00N	85.00W
Ontario, Lake @	50	43.45N	78.00W
Oregon □³	50	44.00N	121.00W
Orinoco ≃	42	8.37N	62.15W
Orkney Islands II	6	59.00N	3.00W
Ōsaka	22	34.40N	135.30 E
Oslo	7	59.55N	10.45 E
Ottawa	52	45.25N	75.42W
Ouagadougou	30	12.22N	1.31W

P

Name	Page No.	Lat.	Long.
Pacific Ocean ▼¹	2	10.00S	150.00W
Pakistan □¹	28	30.00N	70.00 E
Palermo	14	38.07N	13.21 E
Palestine □⁹	29	32.00N	35.15 E
Panamá	44	8.58N	79.32W
Panama □¹	44	9.00N	80.00W
Papua New Guinea □¹	2	6.00S	143.00 E
Paraguay □¹	41	23.00S	58.00W
Paramaribo	42	5.50N	55.10W
Paris	10	48.52N	2.20 E
Peking → Beijing	20	39.55N	116.25 E
Pennsylvania □³	50	40.45N	77.30W
Persian Gulf c	34	27.00N	51.00 E
Peru □¹	42	10.00S	76.00W
Philadelphia	52	39.57N	75.09W
Philippines □¹	24	13.00N	122.00 E
Phnum Pénh	26	11.33N	104.55 E
Phoenix	50	33.26N	112.04W
Pierre	50	44.22N	100.21W
Pikes Peak ▲	50	38.51N	105.03W
Pittsburgh	52	40.26N	79.59W
Pointe-à-Pitre	44	16.14N	61.32W
Poland □¹	4	52.00N	19.00 E
Port-au-Prince	44	18.32N	72.20W
Portland	50	45.31N	122.40W
Port Louis	32	20.10S	57.30 E
Port Moresby	36	9.30S	147.10 E
Porto	12	41.11N	8.36W
Port of Spain	44	10.39N	61.31W
Porto-Novo	30	6.29N	2.37 E
Portugal □¹	4	39.30N	8.00W
Poznań	8	52.25N	16.55 E
Prague → Praha	8	50.05N	14.26 E
Praha (Prague)	8	50.05N	14.26 E
Pretoria	32	25.45S	28.10 E
Prince Edward Island □⁴	48	46.20N	63.20W
Providence	52	41.49N	71.24W
Puerto Rico □²	44	18.15N	66.30W
Pusan	20	35.06N	129.03 E
P'yŏngyang	20	39.01N	125.45 E